6

Wonderful WORLD

SECOND EDITION

GRAMMAR BOOK

T0349566

NATIONAL GEOGRAPHIC
LEARNING

Australia · Brazil · Mexico · Singapore · United Kingdom · United States

Contents

2

Contents

Used to

We use **used to** to talk about
- actions that we often did in the past but we no longer do.
  I used to walk to school every day, but now I cycle.
- situations that existed in the past but don't exist now.
  My uncle used to live in Australia.

Used to is followed by the infinitive of the main verb without **to** (bare infinitive).
My cousins used to play football every weekend.

In the negative form, we use **did**, the word **not, use to** and the bare infinitive.
I didn't use to play baseball.

In the question form, we use **did, use to** and the bare infinitive. In short answers, we only use **did**. We don't use the main verb.
Did you use to play basketball? Yes, I did.

Remember !

We can use **there used to be** to talk about situations in the past.
There used to be more parks in the city.

1 Circle the correct words.

1 I **used / used to** play basketball every weekend.

2 Did you **used to / use to** live in the countryside?

3 I didn't **used to / use to** like tomatoes.

4 **Did he use to / Has he use to** go to our school?

5 There **didn't use to / wasn't used to** be a train station in our town.

6 Mobile phones **use to / used to** be big and heavy.

Ever, never and yet

We use **ever** in questions to ask about things that have happened up to now.
Have you ever visited a nature reserve?

We use **yet** in negative sentences and in questions when we mean *until now*.
Have you tidied your room yet?
I haven't done my homework yet.

We use **never** to talk about things that haven't happened until now. We use **never** in affirmative sentences, but it has a negative meaning.
I've never been to Peru.

Remember !

The word **ever** goes before the past participle and the word **yet** goes at the end of the sentence.
Have you **ever** been to Paris?
We haven't had lunch **yet**.

2 Put the words in the correct order to make sentences.

1 ? / ever / you / eaten / Thai food / have
   Have you ever eaten Thai food?

2 she / seen / the new film / hasn't / yet
   _____

3 never / has / my mum / a horse / ridden
   _____

4 ? / Pavel / has / failed / ever / an English exam
   _____

5 sister / my / finished / hasn't / yet / her breakfast
   _____

6 I've / late / been / never / for school
   _____

For, since, already, just

We use **for** to talk about a period of time and **since** to show when something started in the past.
*I've lived here **for** three years.*
*He has worked at the college **since** 2017.*

We use **already** to show that something has happened and **just** to talk about a recent event.
*I've **already** seen that film.*
*Sara has **just** found her phone.*

3 **Match.**

1 I've lived in this town	**a** I've already seen that film.
2 I don't want to go to the cinema;	**b** for three hours!
3 My mum's been waiting for me since	**c** five years.
4 My brother has been watching TV	**d** since I was four.
5 I wanted to go to the park, but	**e** ten o'clock.
6 She's been studying English for	**f** it's just started raining.

Be going to

We use **be going to**
• to talk about future plans and intentions.
*We**'re going to visit** the zoo on Saturday.*
• to predict that something is going to happen when we have some proof or some information.
*Look at those dark clouds. It**'s going to** rain.*

Be going to is followed by the bare infinitive.
*My brother and I **are going to make** a cake this afternoon.*

4 **Complete the sentences with *be going to*. Use the verbs in brackets.**

1 Look at the sky! It _____'s/is going to rain_____ soon. (rain)

2 I _____ TV tonight. (not watch)

3 My friends _____ to the cinema tonight. (go)

4 Oh no! I woke up late! I _____ my train. (miss)

5 _____ they _____
the Acropolis when they go to Greece next summer? (visit)

6 I _____ a vet when I'm older. (be)

Can, could, be able to

We use **can** to
- show ability in the present.
  I can run very fast.
- ask or give permission for something.
  Can we go outside?
- talk about what is possible.
  We can walk in the park every morning.
- ask somebody to do something for us.
  Can you buy some milk for me, please?

We use **could** to
- talk about ability in the past.
  Rick could swim when he was four years old.
- ask permission for something in the present or the future.
  Could I go to the café with my friends?

- ask for something politely.
  Could I have a glass of water, please?

We don't use **could** for abilities in the past when we talk about a specific occasion when we managed to do something. In this case we use **was able to** or **were able to**.
He was able to solve the problem.

We use **be able to** to talk about
- ability.
  Jane is able to run ten kilometres.
- a specific occasion when we managed or didn't manage to do something.
  I wasn't able to buy the train tickets this morning.

5 Circle the correct answers.

1 **Can** / **Are you able** you pass me the salt, please?
2 **Could / Can** you speak English when you were five?
3 I got up early yesterday, so I **was able to / can** catch the first bus.
4 We **can / could** go to the beach every day when we go on holiday.
5 My cousin **can't / could** see very well. He needs glasses.
6 It's been raining all day. I **haven't been able to / could** take any good photos yet.

See and think

See and **think** are stative verbs. Their meaning changes when they are used with the present continuous.

When the verb **see** means *see* or *understand*, we use the **present simple**.
Mum is home. I see her car.
'You need to turn on your computer here.' 'I see.'

When the verb **see** means *meet* or *visit*, we use the **present simple** and the **present continuous** (future meaning).
I see my sister every day.
I'm seeing my cousin tonight.

When the verb **think** means *have an opinion*, we use the **present simple**.
I think the new film is fantastic!

When the verb **think** means *consider*, we use the **present continuous**.
I'm thinking about where to go tonight.

6 Complete the sentences with the present simple or the present continuous. Use the verbs in brackets.

1 I _____'m/am seeing_____ my grandparents this weekend. (see)

2 We _____ about going to the new café tomorrow. (think)

3 Mum _____ about buying a new car. (think)

4 I _____ what you mean about the new TV programme. It's so funny! (see)

5 What _____ about at the moment? (you, think)

6 Sammy _____ basketball is the best sport in the world. (think)

May, might, must, mustn't, can't

We use **may** and **might** to say that it is possible that something will happen.
*I **may** go to Italy next month.*
*Paul **might** come to the sports centre with us.*

We use **must** to
- say that we are sure that something is true.
  *He **must** be tired. He went to bed really late.*
- talk about obligation.
  *She **must** do her homework before she watches TV.*
- talk about necessity.
  *We **must** do more exercise.*

We use **mustn't** to talk about something that we are not allowed to do in the present and in the future.
*I **mustn't** forget to take my medicine.*
*They **mustn't** make so much noise in the library.*

We use **can't** to say that we are sure that something is not true.
*That **can't** be the new teacher. He doesn't start work until next week.*

7 Choose the correct answers.

1 I _____ stay up late tonight. I need to get up early tomorrow.
   a might
   b must
   c mustn't *(circled)*

2 She looks just like you. She _____ be your sister.
   a can't
   b must
   c might

3 It's really cold; it _____ snow later.
   a might
   b mustn't
   c must

4 She looks very fit. She _____ be an athlete.
   a must
   b can't
   c mustn't

5 They woke up late. They _____ miss their train.
   a can't
   b must
   c might

6 He didn't study enough for his exam. He _____ pass.
   a might not
   b mustn't
   c can't

Passive voice

We use the passive voice when
- we want to emphasise the action rather than who does it.
  *The school **is cleaned** every day.*
- we don't know who does the action.
  *The castle **was built** 400 years ago.*
- it's obvious who does the action.
  *School uniform **is worn** at this school.*

We form the passive voice with the auxiliary verb **be** and the past participle of the main verb. We can use different tenses with the passive voice, but not the present perfect continuous, the past perfect continuous or the future continuous.

8 Complete the sentences with the correct form of the passive voice. Use the verbs in brackets.

1 The concert ___will be performed___ in the park next summer. (perform)

2 The rubbish _____ tomorrow. (not collect)

3 _____ the school _____ yesterday? (clean)

4 The thief _____ yet, but the police are confident that they will find him soon. (not arrest)

5 A lot of wildlife _____ by the flood last month. (destroyed)

6 Our glass bottles _____ every week. (recycle)

1 **Read.**

Lucy lives in New York. Today she's taking a taxi to the Upper East Side.

Present simple

We use the **present simple** to talk about
- general truths.
  *People in Brazil **speak** Portuguese.*
- things that we do regularly.
  *My cousin and I **go** to the park every Saturday.*
- permanent situations.
  *We **live** in New York City.*
- timetabled and programmed events in the future.
  *The auction **begins** at five o'clock in the afternoon.*

Time expressions
The following **time expressions** go at the beginning or at the end of a sentence: **every day, at the weekend, in the morning, on Mondays, in January, on Friday evenings, twice a week,** etc.

Adverbs of frequency
We use **adverbs of frequency** when we want to say how frequently something happens.

The following **adverbs of frequency** go before the main verb but after the verb **be: never, rarely, sometimes, often, usually, regularly, frequently, always.**
*Natalie **always hands in** her assignments on time.*
*James **is never** late for an appointment.*

We use **How often ...?** to ask about how frequently something happens.
***How often** do you go to the dentist?*
Twice a year.

Affirmative	Negative	Question	Short answers	
I work	I don't work	Do I work ...?	Yes, I do.	No, I don't.
you work	you don't work	Do you work ...?	Yes, you do.	No, you don't.
he works	he doesn't work	Does he work ...?	Yes, he does.	No, he doesn't.
she works	she doesn't work	Does she work ...?	Yes, she does.	No, she doesn't.
it works	it doesn't work	Does it work ...?	Yes, it does.	No, it doesn't.
we work	we don't work	Do we work ...?	Yes, we do.	No, we don't.
you work	you don't work	Do you work ...?	Yes, you do.	No, you don't.
they work	they don't work	Do they work ...?	Yes, they do.	No, they don't.

2 Complete the sentences with the correct form of the present simple. Use the verbs in brackets.

1 Dad and I often _____ make _____ noodles for lunch. (make)

2 My favourite football player _____ goals very often. (not score)

3 _____ you _____ your friends at the weekends? (meet)

4 Paula always _____ her hair before she goes out. (brush)

5 Timothy _____ his suitcase by himself. (not pack)

6 Karen always _____ to do the best she can. (try)

7 _____ the celebrity _____ in an apartment in Manhattan? (live)

8 The cat _____ all its milk. (not drink)

Present continuous

We use the **present continuous** to talk about
- actions that are in progress at the time of speaking.
  *The local department store **is selling** all designer clothes at 50% off today!*
- actions that are in progress around the time of speaking.
  *They **are redecorating** the Beverly Hills Hotel.*
- actions that are temporary.
  *Susan **is working** from home these days.*
- future plans that we have arranged; they usually refer to the near future.
  *We**'re visiting** the National Gallery this Friday.*
- annoying habits (with **always**, **constantly**, **forever**).
  *Jodie **is constantly forgetting** her homework!*
- changing situations.
  *Your little brother **is growing** taller and taller every day.*
- what is happening in a picture or photograph.
  *The celebrity and her children **are enjoying** a walk in the park in this photo.*

Time expressions
We often use the following **time expressions** with the **present continuous: now, right now, at the moment, for the time being, today, these days, this morning/afternoon/week/year,** etc.
*John is washing his bike **at the moment**.*
*Sue is taking the bus to work **these days**.*

Affirmative	Negative	Question	Short answers	
I'm staying	I'm not staying	Am I staying ...?	Yes, I am.	No, I'm not.
you're staying	you aren't staying	Are you staying ...?	Yes, you are.	No, you aren't.
he's staying	he isn't staying	Is he staying ...?	Yes, he is.	No, he isn't.
she's staying	she isn't staying	Is she staying ...?	Yes, she is.	No, she isn't.
it's staying	it isn't staying	Is it staying ...?	Yes, it is.	No, it isn't.
we're staying	we aren't staying	Are we staying ...?	Yes, we are.	No, we aren't.
you're staying	you aren't staying	Are you staying ...?	Yes, you are.	No, you aren't.
they're staying	they aren't staying	Are they staying ...?	Yes, they are.	No, they aren't.

3 Complete the sentences with the correct form of the present continuous. Use the words in brackets.

1 The weather _____ is getting _____ warmer and warmer these days. (get)

2 Gregory _____ in a hotel because he prefers camping. (not stay)

3 I can't come with you. I _____ for a maths test at the moment. (study)

4 _____ lunch with your colleagues tomorrow? (you / have)

5 My little brother _____ with my toys. (forever play)

6 _____ Grandma tomorrow? (they / visit)

4 Look at the pictures and complete the sentences with the correct form of the present continuous. Use these verbs.

~~audition~~   enjoy   interview   listen   sign   watch

1 At the moment, Julia ___is auditioning___ for the reality show.

2 This week, my favourite author _____ autographs for her new book.

3 Mandy and her sister _____ a film this afternoon.

4 _____ you and your friends _____ yourselves?

5 The journalist _____ the gold medallist right now.

6 _____ Sandra _____ to music?

5 Circle the correct words.

1 Our train to Milan **departs** / **is departing** at eight o'clock tomorrow morning.

2 For the time being, the famous sculptor **works** / **is working** in San Francisco.

3 The local theatrical group **performs** / **is performing** every Friday evening in the park.

4 Dad is a journalist, but he rarely **interviews** / **is interviewing** famous people.

5 In this photo my sister **plays** / **is playing** tennis.

6 Our school **has** / **is having** a book sale in the library next week.

6 Match.

1 Does your school frequently raise money for charity?   **a** No, she doesn't.

2 Are you travelling around Australia next month?   **b** Yes, I am.

3 Do newspapers always publish articles about the rich and famous?   **c** Yes, it does.

4 Is the local football team playing on this pitch tomorrow?   **d** Yes, they are.

5 Are Freddie and Jane staying in their cousin's flat for the time being?   **e** No, it isn't.

6 Does your mother work in a bank?   **f** No, they don't.

7 **Choose the correct answers.**

1 _____ with your family at the weekend?
  a Do you often go away
  b Are you often going away
  c You often go away

2 It's so annoying. My neighbours _____ a lot of noise.
  a are making always
  b are always making
  c always makes

3 At the moment, the actor _____ for her new role.
  a rehearse
  b rehearsing
  c is rehearsing

4 _____ the best performer at the end of the competition every year?
  a Does the judge choose
  b Is the judge choosing
  c Is the judge choose

5 The party _____ until nine o'clock at night.
  a doesn't start
  b is starting
  c starts

6 The price of petrol _____ more and more every day!
  a increase
  b is increasing
  c increasing

8 **Complete the telephone conversation with the present simple or the present continuous. Use the words in brackets.**

Isabel: What's the matter, Dan?

Dan: It's my brother. He (1) ___is constantly hiding___ (constantly hide) my games.

Isabel: Oh dear. Listen, our favourite R & B group (2) _____ (go) on tour in a few months. Shall we get tickets?

Dan: I (3) _____ (not know). Our teacher (4) _____ (forever give) us lots of homework, and the concert (5) _____ (not end) until late.

Isabel: True, but we (6) _____ (not get) the chance to see them often.

Dan: You're right. And they (7) _____ (record) their new album at the moment.

Isabel: (8) _____ then? (you / agree)

Dan: Yes!

9 **Say it! Look at the pictures and talk with your partner about how often you do these things. Use appropriate adverbs of frequency and time expressions.**

I usually exercise every Saturday morning.

I always walk to school with my friends.

1 **Read.**

These flowers smell great!

Stative verbs

Stative verbs describe states, not actions. We don't usually use **stative verbs** with continuous tenses, such as the **present continuous**. The most common **stative verbs** are:

verbs of senses:
feel, hear, see, smell, sound, taste
*These noodles **taste** awful!*

verbs of emotion:
dislike, hate, like, love, need, prefer, want
*I **prefer** jeans to formal trousers.*

verbs of understanding and opinion:
appear, believe, forget, hope, imagine, know, mean, realise, remember, seem, think, understand, wonder
*Alice never **remembers** her email password.*

verbs that show possession:
belong to, have, own, possess
*This book **belongs to** John.*

Some **stative verbs** can be used with the **present continuous**, but their meaning changes.
These verbs include:
appear, be, feel, have, look, see, think

*The actor **appears** to be tired. (He looks tired.)*
*The jazz band **is appearing** at the local pub this weekend. (The band is performing.)*

*Penny went to bed because she **has** a bad headache. (Her head hurts.)*
*I**'m having** lunch at the moment. (I am eating lunch now.)*

*I **feel** happy about my success. (I am glad that I am successful.)*
*Sue **is feeling** the fabric to see if she likes it. (She is touching it.)*

*Jason **looks** really happy today. (He appears to be happy.)*
*What **are** you **looking** at? (What are you watching?)*

***Do** you **see** the rainbow in the sky? (Are you able to see it?)*
*I**'m seeing** my old classmates this Saturday. (I have an appointment.)*

*Mrs Jones **thinks** that we should study every night. (She believes this.)*
*My parents **are thinking** of buying a new car. (They are considering this.)*

2 Complete the sentences with the present simple or the present continuous. Use the verbs in brackets.

1 I _____ hear _____ what you're saying, but I don't agree. (hear)

2 _____ what I am saying? (you / understand)

3 Melinda _____ at the moment. She's looking for a new job. (not work)

4 This is such a nice T-shirt. I _____ it! (love)

5 The children are so happy. They _____ a wonderful time. (have)

6 It's not my book. I _____ it. (not own)

7 We can either go to the park or to the sports centre. What _____? (you / prefer)

8 I _____ about anything at the moment. (not think)

3 Write sentences with the present simple or the present continuous.

1 Fiona / dislike / comedies / and / musicals
   Fiona dislikes comedies and musicals.

2 Harriet / appear / in / a West End musical / next month
   _____

3 ? / you / remember / when / we met
   _____

4 ? / you / meet / the director / tomorrow morning
   _____

5 Lionel Messi / be / a very good football player
   _____

6 my brother / constantly / forget / my birthday
   _____

4 Complete the sentences with the present simple or the present continuous. Use these verbs.

(~~have~~   look   not like   not think   see   think)

1 The musicians _____ are having _____ dinner with the songwriter this evening.

2 This portrait _____ great in the living room.

3 Carrie _____ a doctor this afternoon about her broken arm.

4 I _____ the first track on this album is too bad.

5 I _____ this soup!

6 We _____ of going to the awards ceremony later this afternoon.

5 Complete the advertisement with the present simple or the present continuous. Use the verbs in brackets.

Dreams do come true!

(1) _____ Do _____ you _____ believe _____ (believe) in dreams coming true?

(2) _____ you _____ (want) to start a career?

We (3) _____ (look for) talented actors between 17 and 24 years old.

All you (4) _____ (need) is a good voice and the will to succeed.

If you (5) _____ (think) you're ready for stardom, we
(6) _____ (see) performers from all over the country next week.

Contact us on 0800 230970.

6 Complete the dialogue with the present simple or the present continuous. Use these verbs.

> love   not like   own   prefer   see   sound   ~~want~~

Henrietta: George, (1) _____do_____ you _____want_____ to do something different this summer?

George: Mm. That (2) _____ interesting!

Henrietta: There's a great music festival in June.

George: Wow! I absolutely (3) _____ music! Yes, let's go!

Henrietta: Great. Let's book our flights.

George: Flights? Oh, maybe not. I (4) _____ flying. It's scary.

Henrietta: I (5) _____ what you mean.

George: I (6) _____ going to festivals in England.

Henrietta: Well, there's a traditional music festival in Cambridge.

George: Great! My family (7) _____ a house in Cambridge. We can stay there!

7 Say it! Talk to your partner about what you would say in these situations. Use stative verbs.

> You are talking to a new friend about what you like and don't like.

> You tried a new dish and you are describing it to your mum.

> Your teacher has asked the class to tell him your opinions about recycling.

> I really like traditional music.

> Actually, I prefer classical music.

1 **Read.**

Direct and indirect objects

Some sentences have two objects, a direct object and an indirect object. The direct object is the person, animal or thing to which the verb relates or the action is done. The indirect object is the person, animal or thing which can receive the direct object or to whom the direct object is given. We can usually identify the **direct object** by asking **what**. If the direct object is a person, we can identify it by asking **who**.

My parents bought me a new computer.
Q: **What** did my parents buy?
A: a **new computer** (direct object)

My dad took me to the party.
Q: **Who** did your dad take to the party?
A: **me** (direct object)

We can identify the **indirect object** by asking the questions **for/to whom** or **for/to what**.

My parents bought me a new computer.
Q: **For whom** did they buy it?
A: **me** (indirect object)

My dad took me to the party.
Q: **To what** did your dad take you?
A: **the party** (indirect object)

The **indirect object** always comes before the **direct object** in a sentence.
*Jane gave **Mark** a blue **T-shirt**.*
*Mum made **me** a fantastic **birthday cake**.*

We can also write these sentences using a prepositional phrase with **to** or **for**.
*Jane gave a blue **T-shirt to Mark**.*
*Mum made a fantastic **birthday cake for me**.*

However, sentences which use verbs such as **ask** and **cost** cannot be rewritten using a prepositional phrase.
I asked my mother a question.
The painting cost Jane a lot of money.

2 **Underline the direct objects and circle the indirect objects.**

1   The director offered (me) the <u>part</u>.

2   The actor showed us a white rabbit.

3   The fans sent the actor emails.

4   Dad bought Mum some flowers.

5   I gave my sister a fresh sweet apple.

6   The tourist lent me his camera.

7   I wrote my family a postcard.

8   Her parents gave her a car for her birthday.

3 **Rewrite the sentences using a prepositional phrase with *to* or *for*.**

1   Dad bought us a huge carton of popcorn.
    <u>Dad bought a huge carton of popcorn for us.</u>

2   Our school always gives poverty-stricken children money.
    _____

3   Serena told her friends a hilarious joke.
    _____

4   I've already given you three of my new games!
    _____

5   We showed the tourists Mount al-Mokattam.
    _____

6   Did you bring me the theatre tickets?
    _____

7   My sister made me a lovely birthday card.
    _____

8   Peter gave Ben a new game.
    _____

4 **Find the mistakes and write the sentences correctly.**

1   Harry is buying a watch his mother.
    <u>Harry is buying a watch for his mother/his mother a watch.</u>

2   Daddy! Daddy! Buy for me some sweets!
    _____

3   The bank manager is going to send a reply me.
    _____

4   Will showed us to the stars through his telescope.
    _____

5   My penfriend sends to me a letter every month.
    _____

6   We made a beautiful leaving card to our teacher.
    _____

5 **Put the words in the correct order to write sentences.**

1 is / ball / me / throwing / to / he / the
   <u>He is throwing the ball to me.</u>

2 tonight / you / for / am / I / paying
   _____

3 a difficult question / asked / Mr Ledson / me
   _____

4 are / they / us / dinner / cooking
   _____

5 homework / gives / your / a lot of / teacher / you
   _____

6 on / you / spend / much / too / games / money
   _____

7 they / car / him / are / their / showing
   _____

8 didn't cost / my / me / a lot of money / new laptop
   _____

6 **Say it! Look at the cards with a partner and use the prompts to talk about these situations.**

Mum's birthday
buy / flowers / her
make / a birthday cake
cook / dinner

Playing football
a friend / explained /
the rules / me
kick / the ball / me
pass / the ball / a friend

In class
Mrs Ball / read / a story / us
show / us / an interesting film
sing / songs / us

I buy my mum flowers for her birthday.

We make a birthday cake for Mum.

1 Read.

We climbed Mount Everest last year! In fact, this time last year, we were arriving at Base Camp.

Past simple

We use the **past simple** to talk about
- actions that started and finished in the past.
  *Peter **won** the 100-metre race yesterday.*
- past habits.
  *I **watched** cartoons every Saturday morning when I was younger.*
- actions that happened one after the other in the past.
  *Andrew **climbed** to the top of the mountain, **looked** around and **took** a picture of the view.*

Time expressions
The following **time expressions** are used with the **past simple: yesterday, the day before yesterday, the other day, last week, a week ago, in January, in 2017, last summer, on 21st April,** etc.
*I went on an excursion **the day before yesterday**.*
*My grandparents went on a cruise **last week**.*

Affirmative	Negative	Question	Short answers	
I finished	I didn't finish	Did I finish ...?	Yes, I did.	No, I didn't.
you finished	you didn't finish	Did you finish ...?	Yes, you did.	No, you didn't.
he finished	he didn't finish	Did he finish ...?	Yes, he did.	No, he didn't.
she finished	she didn't finish	Did she finish ...?	Yes, she did.	No, she didn't.
it finished	it didn't finish	Did it finish ...?	Yes, it did.	No, it didn't.
we finished	we didn't finish	Did we finish ...?	Yes, we did.	No, we didn't.
you finished	you didn't finish	Did you finish ...?	Yes, you did.	No, you didn't.
they finished	they didn't finish	Did they finish ...?	Yes, they did.	No, they didn't.

See the Irregular verbs list on page 159.

2 Complete the sentences with the past simple. Use the verbs in brackets.

1 When Dalia was ten years old, she _____painted_____ her first portrait. (paint)

2 Last year, Thomas _____ for two months in Cambridge at Summer School. (study)

3 Henry VI _____ King of England in 1422. (become)

4 Two years ago, we _____ around Europe. (drive)

5 My little brother _____ all his toy dinosaurs in the park this morning. (lose)

6 We _____ our suitcases, _____ the car and _____ on our journey. (pack, get in, set off)

Past continuous

We use the **past continuous**
- to talk about an action that was in progress at a specific time in the past.
  *At three o'clock yesterday afternoon, we **were walking** through Hyde Park.*
- to talk about two or more actions that were in progress at the same time in the past. We use **and** or **while** to connect the actions.
  *I **was writing** an email **and** Jessie **was speaking** to her cousin on Skype.*
  *Nancy **was watching** a film **while** Peter **was making** sandwiches.*
- to describe the scene of a story.
  *The sun **was shining**, the children **were playing** in the garden and their parents **were chatting**.*
- to talk about an action that was in progress in the past that was interrupted by another action.
  *We **were listening** when the music stopped.*

Time expressions
We often use the following **time expressions** with the **past continuous: all morning, all day yesterday, at six o'clock, last year, this morning, this time last week, from nine to five,** etc.
*My parents were painting my bedroom **all day yesterday**.*
*I was playing tennis **this morning**.*

Affirmative	Negative	Question	Short answers	
I was sleeping	I wasn't sleeping	Was I sleeping ...?	Yes, I was.	No, I wasn't.
you were sleeping	you weren't sleeping	Were you sleeping ...?	Yes, you were.	No, you weren't.
he was sleeping	he wasn't sleeping	Was he sleeping ...?	Yes, he was.	No, he wasn't.
she was sleeping	she wasn't sleeping	Was she sleeping ...?	Yes, she was.	No, she wasn't.
it was sleeping	it wasn't sleeping	Was it sleeping ...?	Yes, it was.	No, it wasn't.
we were sleeping	we weren't sleeping	Were we sleeping ...?	Yes, we were.	No, we weren't.
you were sleeping	you weren't sleeping	Were you sleeping ...?	Yes, you were.	No, you weren't.
they were sleeping	they weren't sleeping	Were they sleeping ...?	Yes, they were.	No, they weren't.

3 Complete the sentences with the past continuous. Use these verbs.

drive   not sail   pack   play   read   shine   sing   sleep   ~~walk~~   watch

1 I _____was walking_____ home when it started to rain.

2 _____ you _____ your suitcases all last night?

3 At eight o'clock last night, the twins _____ an adventure film.

4 Last summer, we _____ around the Greek islands.

5 My little brother _____ with his dinosaurs all morning.

6 During the trip, Nancy _____ the car and I _____ the map.

7 It was a glorious day! The birds _____ and the sun _____ .

8 _____ Munir_____ when you called him this morning?

Past simple and past continuous

We use the **past simple** and the **past continuous** in the same sentence when
- an action that was in progress in the past was interrupted by another action.
  *We **were watching** a film when our cousins **arrived**.*
- we tell a story in the past.
  *I **was walking** down the street when I **bumped into** Angela.*

4 Complete Tracey's diary entry with the past simple or the past continuous. Use the verbs in brackets.

Yesterday, I had a great day! I woke up, got dressed and (1) _____left_____ (leave) home at half past eight. While I (2) _____ (walk) to school, I met my friend Jenny. It was the day of the school trip to the archaeological museum and we (3) _____ (be) very excited.

When we (4) _____ (get) to school, the bus was leaving so we ran to catch it! The journey to the museum was fun, too. While the bus driver (5) _____ (drive), we were talking to our friends.

At the museum, we (6) _____ (see) beautiful sculptures and vases. While we (7) _____ (admire) the exhibits, Jenny shouted 'Look!' and she ran towards the Egyptian art collection.

I (8) _____ (try) to find Jenny when I saw our favourite actor. Jenny was standing next to him. She was giving him a pen and he was smiling at her! Jenny was so happy because he gave her his autograph.

As, when, while

We usually use **as, when** and **while** to connect two actions.

We use **as/when** before the **past simple**
- to refer to two short actions which happened at the same time.
  ***As** I opened my eyes, I saw a bright light.*

We use **when** before the **past simple** for
- a short action that interrupted a long action.
  *They were having dinner **when** the phone rang.*
- a short action that happened immediately after another short action.
  *I caught the ball **when** Joe threw it.*

We also use **when** to talk about
- a person's age when something happened.
  ***When** Vicky was five, she went to school.*
- a period of a person's life when something happened.
  ***When** Ricky was at school, he won a skateboarding competition.*

We usually use **while** before the **past continuous** to talk about
- two long actions that were happening at the same time.
  *Jake was watching a film **while** his sister was tidying her room.*

We usually use **as/while** before the **past continuous** to talk about
- a long action that was happening when a short action interrupted it.
  ***As/While** Julie was walking home, it started to rain.*

5 **Complete the sentences with *as, when* or *while*.**

1 It was pouring with rain _____ when _____ the sun came out.

2 _____ Frank put down the phone, the electricity went off.

3 Janet fell off her bike _____ she was cycling to work.

4 _____ I was locking the front door, I dropped my keys.

5 We were watching the World Cup on TV _____ Brazil scored a goal.

6 _____ you were sleeping, your little sister was playing games on your computer.

7 _____ Sara was ten, she got a pet cat.

8 I was looking through the trunk _____ I came across Grandma's old possessions.

6 **Write sentences with the past simple and/or the past continuous.**

1 we / admire / the sculptures / when / the lights go / out
   We were admiring the sculptures when the lights went out.

2 as / I jog / along the beach / I catch / a glimpse of / a famous celebrity
   _____

3 ? / Natalie / watch / TV / when / the taxi / arrive
   _____

4 John / take / photos / of the Eiffel Tower / while / Judy / choose / postcards
   _____

5 ? / you / write / an email / when / you / drop / your laptop
   _____

6 Mr and Mrs Long / sleep / when / they / hear / a loud noise
   _____

7 as / the children / swim / they / see / a shark
   _____

8 the football player / talk / to his fans / while / he / sign / autographs
   _____

7 **Complete the text with the past simple or the past continuous. Use the verbs in brackets.**

The *Titanic* (1) _____ was _____ (be) the largest passenger ship in the world at the time of its construction. It (2) _____ (begin) its voyage on 10th April 1912, but it never (3) _____ (reach) its destination.

What (4) _____ (happen) on the night of the disaster? Just before midnight, as the ship (5) _____ (sail), two members of the crew (6) _____ (see) a huge iceberg directly in front of the ship. They (7) _____ (try) to change the ship's course, but the iceberg was too close. The *Titanic* (8) _____ (hit) the iceberg and the side of the ship was badly damaged. This caused the ship to start flooding.

While the crew (9) _____ (help) passengers into the lifeboats, the captain tried to get help. Unfortunately, the *Titanic* (10) _____ (not carry) enough lifeboats for everyone on board, so many people died.

8 Say it! Look at Josh and Kelly's diary with your partner. Ask and answer questions about what Josh and Kelly did on Saturday.

	JOSH		KELLY	
8 a.m.	woke up		was asleep	
12 p.m.	watched documentary about Peru		went to shops to look for costume for party	
2 p.m.	had lunch with Dad		visited Natural History Museum	
4 p.m.	surfed the Internet for information about pyramids		rang Josh	
8 p.m.	read comics		got ready for party	
12 a.m.	was asleep		came back from party	

What time did Josh wake up?

What was Kelly doing at eight o'clock in the morning?

He woke up at eight o'clock.

She was sleeping.

1 **Read.**

When I was a young boy, I used to play chess with my grandad.

Yes, you did. He would always let you win!

Used to

We use **used to** to talk about
• actions that we often did in the past but we no longer do.
  *I **used to enjoy** playing board games.*
• situations that existed in the past but don't exist now.
  *My family and I **used to live** in a cottage.*

Used to is followed by the infinitive of the main verb without **to** (bare infinitive).
*Rebecca **used to ride** her bike to school.*

Remember!

We can use **didn't use to** to talk about actions or states that happen often or exist now, but that didn't in the past.
*My friends and I **didn't use to send** text messages.* (but we do now)

Affirmative	Negative	Question	Short answers	
I used to enjoy	I didn't use to enjoy	Did I use to enjoy ...?	Yes, I did.	No, I didn't.
you used to enjoy	you didn't use to enjoy	Did you use to enjoy ...?	Yes, you did.	No, you didn't.
he used to enjoy	he didn't use to enjoy	Did he use to enjoy ...?	Yes, he did.	No, he didn't.
she used to enjoy	she didn't use to enjoy	Did she use to enjoy ...?	Yes, she did.	No, she didn't.
it used to enjoy	it didn't use to enjoy	Did it use to enjoy ...?	Yes, it did.	No, it didn't.
we used to enjoy	we didn't use to enjoy	Did we use to enjoy ...?	Yes, we did.	No, we didn't.
you used to enjoy	you didn't use to enjoy	Did you use to enjoy ...?	Yes, you did.	No, you didn't.
they used to enjoy	they didn't use to enjoy	Did they use to enjoy ...?	Yes, they did.	No, they didn't.

2 **Complete the sentences with the correct form of *used to*. Use the verbs in brackets.**

1 In Spain, bullfighting _____used to be_____ a sport for the aristocracy. (be)

2 The Berlin Wall _____ East and West Germany. (separate)

3 We _____ the Internet at home, so I couldn't do research online. (not have)

4 _____ you _____ to school by yourself? (walk)

5 Jeremy_____ basketball, but now he does. (not play)

6 _____ Katy and Isabel _____ a room at university? (share)

Would

We use **would** to talk about actions that we often did in the past but we no longer do.
*We **would** always go to school by bus.*

We can't use **would** to talk about states in the past, and we don't usually use the negative
form (wouldn't).

Affirmative	Negative	Question	Short answers	
I would visit	I wouldn't visit	Would I visit ...?	Yes, I would.	No, I wouldn't.
you would visit	you wouldn't visit	Would you visit ...?	Yes, you would.	No, you wouldn't.
he would visit	he wouldn't visit	Would he visit ...?	Yes, he would.	No, he wouldn't.
she would visit	she wouldn't visit	Would she visit ...?	Yes, she would.	No, she wouldn't.
it would visit	it wouldn't visit	Would it visit ...?	Yes, it would.	No, it wouldn't.
we would visit	we wouldn't visit	Would we visit ...?	Yes, we would.	No, we wouldn't.
you would visit	you wouldn't visit	Would you visit ...?	Yes, you would.	No, you wouldn't.
they would visit	they wouldn't visit	Would they visit ...?	Yes, they would.	No, they wouldn't.

3 Complete the sentences with the correct form of *would*. Use these verbs.

> cry   invite   read   take   ~~tell~~   walk

1 Grandad _____ would _____ always _____ tell _____ us stories about the Second World War.

2 _____ your classmates _____ you to parties?

3 I saw many wonderful sights when I was young because my parents _____ me on many holidays.

4 My little sister _____ all the time when she was a baby.

5 Ryan _____ never _____ science fiction books when he was younger.

6 _____ you always _____ to school when you were younger?

4 Replace the words in bold with *would* where possible.

1 **Did** I **use to** like noodles when I was younger? _____

2 Joseph **used to** guess the ending of every film we saw. _____

3 The film star **didn't use to** be so stunning. _____

4 Our football team **used to** often win the championship. _____

5 **Did** you **use to** read magazines when you were younger? _____

6 A decade ago, there **didn't use to** be so many blocks of flats in my neighbourhood. _____

5 Circle the correct words.

1 Wendy (used to) / would live in Madrid.

2 My friends and I **didn't used / would** play in the park after school.

3 My mum **would / used to** have blonde hair.

4 I **didn't use to / would** like thrillers, but I do now.

5 My brother **would / use to** borrow our dad's car.

6 **Did you use to / Would you** enjoy school when you were younger?

7 My grandma **used / would** go swimming in the sea every morning.

8 My teacher **would / use to** always say 'Sit down and be quiet.'

6 Choose the correct answers.

When I was still at school, my family and I (1) _____ to spend the weekends in the city. We (2) _____ a house in the countryside near a beautiful lake, and we went there every Thursday evening.

On Fridays, Mum and I (3) _____ to go to the village; we (4) _____ stay at home. Dad and Ben, my brother, (5) _____ to go to the local football matches and Ben (6) _____ home a signed copy of his ticket. On Saturdays, we sometimes went sailing and then out for lunch together.

What (7) _____ most? Sailing, but we (8) _____ go sailing if the weather was good.

1	**a** didn't use	**b**	used to	**c**	would
2	**a** used to own	**b**	would own	**c**	use to own
3	**a** not used to	**b**	wouldn't	**c**	didn't use
4	**a** used just to	**b**	would just	**c**	used just
5	**a** would	**b**	used	**c**	use
6	**a** would often bring	**b**	would bring often	**c**	used often bring
7	**a** would like	**b**	we would like	**c**	did we use to like
8	**a** used only	**b**	would only	**c**	did use only

7 Say it! Talk with your partner about how life used to be and what people would do 50 years ago. Use *would*, *used to* and these suggestions to help you.

- people were more relaxed
- cities were less polluted
- children did less homework
- more greenery
- not many supermarkets
- have the Internet
- write letters

Children used to have more free time.

Most people would walk more.

1 Read.

Used to

We use **used to + bare infinitive** to talk about actions that happened often in the past or states that existed in the past but don't now.
*Sandy **used to help** me with my Latin homework.*
*My teacher **used to live** in Japan.*

Remember !

In the negative and question form we use **use to** and not **used to**.

2 Complete the sentences with the correct form of *used to* and the verbs in brackets.

1 Many years ago, explorers ____used to travel____ by ship. (travel)

2 _____ you _____ milk before you went to bed? (drink)

3 At the beginning of the 20th century, many Greeks _____ in Alexandria. (live)

4 _____ your parents _____ by coach or plane? (travel)

5 My mother _____ soap operas, but now she does. (not watch)

6 _____ Steven Gerrard _____ for Liverpool? (play)

7 _____ you _____ Manchester United when you were younger? (support)

8 My brother _____ every time my mother left him. (cry)

Get used to

We use **get used to + –ing** or a noun to talk about actions or states that are becoming familiar to us.

We can use **get used to** with all tenses and with modal verbs.
I'm getting used to wearing a school uniform.
She's getting used to working in a hospital.
We should get used to eating more healthily.
They're getting used to living in the countryside.

Affirmative	Negative	Question	Short answers	
I get used to working	I don't get used to working	Do I get used to working ...?	Yes, I do.	No, I don't.
you get used to working	you don't get used to working	Do you get used to working ...?	Yes, you do.	No, you don't.
he gets used to working	he doesn't get used to working	Does he get used to working ...?	Yes, he does.	No, he doesn't.
she gets used to working	she doesn't get used to working	Does she get used to working ...?	Yes, she does.	No, she doesn't.
it gets used to working	it doesn't get used to working	Does it get used to working ...?	Yes, it does.	No, it doesn't.
we get used to working	we don't get used to working	Do we get used to working ...?	Yes, we do.	No, we don't.
you get used to working	you don't get used to working	Do you get used to working ...?	Yes, you do.	No, you don't.
they get used to working	they don't get used to working	Do they get used to working ...?	Yes, they do.	No, they don't.

3 Complete the sentences using the correct form of *get used to* and these verbs.

> drive   live   speak   use   wake up   ~~work~~

1 After complaining for a year, Dad finally _____<u>got used to working</u>_____ in the city centre.

2 Evan must _____ at seven o'clock in the morning.

3 Hannah _____ a computer yet.

4 It's difficult to _____ in a foreign country.

5 I tried very hard, but I couldn't _____ on the left-hand side of the road.

6 Karim _____ in English now.

4 Write questions using the correct form of *get used to*.

1 <u>Are you getting used to your new routine?</u> _____

Yes, I'm getting used to my new routine.

2 _____

No, we won't get used to living in a remote area.

3 _____

Yes, the new ruler will get used to being in power.

4 _____

No, Tamara and Alex haven't got used to their new Arabic teacher.

5 _____

Yes, you should get used to the residents in this small community.

6 _____

No, Thomas isn't getting used to working in the museum.

Be used to

We use **be used to** + **–ing** or a noun to talk about actions or states that are no longer unusual.

We can use **be used to** with all tenses apart from the continuous tenses and modal verbs.
*Helena **is used to cycling** to work.*
*I **am used to having** cereal for breakfast.*

Affirmative	Negative	Question	Short answers	
I'm used to writing	I'm not used to writing	Am I used to writing ...?	Yes, I am.	No, I'm not.
you're used to writing	you aren't used to writing	Are you used to writing ...?	Yes, you are.	No, you aren't.
he's used to writing	he isn't used to writing	Is he used to writing ...?	Yes, he is.	No, he isn't.
she's used to writing	she isn't used to writing	Is she used to writing ...?	Yes, she is.	No, she isn't.
it's used to writing	it isn't used to writing	Is it used to writing ...?	Yes, it is.	No, it isn't.
we're used to writing	we aren't used to writing	Are we used to writing ...?	Yes, we are.	No, we aren't.
you're used to writing	you aren't used to writing	Are you used to writing ...?	Yes, you are.	No, you aren't.
they're used to writing	they aren't used to writing	Are they used to writing ...?	Yes, they are.	No, they aren't.

5 **Look at the situations and write sentences with the correct form of *be used to*.**

1 Veronica is trying to send an email, but she is having difficulty.

   Veronica isn't used to sending emails.

2 Our mum always cooks healthy food, so we never eat anything else.

   _____

3 When we moved to the country, Dad started cycling to work. It was difficult for him.

   _____

4 These days, most teachers can use interactive whiteboards.

   _____

5 When we lived in England it rained a lot, but it didn't bother us.

   _____

6 I don't go out for lunch during the week.

   _____

6 **Complete the questions using the correct form of *be used to* and then write short answers.**

 **1** ? / Lucy / knit
   Is Lucy used to knitting?
   No, she isn't.
   _____

 **2** ? / Jason / water-skiing
   _____
   _____
   _____

 **3** ? / your grandmother / use / a computer
   _____
   _____
   _____

4 ? / Billy and Neil / write / text messages
   _____
   _____
   _____

 **5** ? / Mr Stevens / fly
   _____
   _____
   _____

 **6** ? / the girls / wear / a school uniform
   _____
   _____
   _____

7 **Match.**

1 Don't be shy! You should get used
2 When I was at boarding school in Kent, I
3 Did Isabella use
4 Now that I'm on a diet,
5 Sophia's mum worked long hours, so Sophia was used to
6 Before she became rich and famous, Gina didn't
7 He's just moved to Greece, so he
8 When Dad was younger, he used

a to go to summer school in England?
b to speaking in front of an audience.
c use to earn a lot of money.
d used to wear a school uniform.
e I'm getting used to eating more fruit and vegetables.
f cooking for herself.
g to live in Hong Kong.
h isn't used to speaking Greek.

8 **Complete the text with the correct form of *used to, get used to, be used to* and the verbs in brackets.**

My classmates and I never (1) _____ used to like _____ (like) history.
We (2) _____ (think) it was boring, as we could never
(3) _____ (learn) dates of important battles and historical events.
Then, six months ago, Mrs Hatton arrived at our school and we slowly
(4) _____ (study) in a different way. She encouraged us to use
small cards and to write dates and a summary of the battle or event on each card.
At the time, we (5) _____ (not make) an
effort, but we all decided to give it a try. Of course, it worked! Now,
we (6) _____ (memorise) the
information on our cards, and the exams are so much easier!

9 **Say it! Imagine that have moved to a foreign country. Talk with your partner about what you have to get used to now and about what you used to do before. Use these suggestions to help you.**

- new school
- learn a foreign language
- different way of life
- speak my language at school
- feel comfortable in my neighbourhood
- have a lot of friends

I am getting used to my new teachers.

I used to know a lot of people.

Review

1 Complete Helen's profile. Use the present simple or the present continuous. Use these verbs.

> be   collect   live   meet   play   speak   travel   work

Who's new in the music world?

Helen Colet (1) _____is_____ from London, England, but at the moment, she (2) _____ in Milan.

She (3) _____ English and Italian, and for the time being, she (4) _____ as a music journalist.

Helen (5) _____ vintage guitars and she (6) _____ basketball every Friday evening.

This weekend, she (7) _____ a famous songwriter for a magazine article that she is writing.

She (8) _____ him in Rome. This summer, Helen (9) _____ to Thailand.

2 Complete the dialogue with the present simple or the present continuous. Use the verbs in brackets.

Stephanie:	(1) _____Do you remember_____ (you / remember) Delia from school?
Sarah:	The girl with the pony?
Stephanie:	That's right. I (2) _____ (see) her this week. (3) _____ (you / want) to come?
Sarah:	Well, I (4) _____ (have got) a lot of homework, so I'm not sure ...
Stephanie:	Anyhow, she (5) _____ (have) a birthday party next weekend. There will be a clown there! Can you come?
Sarah:	Sure! I really (6) _____ (like) birthday parties. I can't wait to see Delia again!
Stephanie:	She (7) _____ (be) still really funny. By the way, she (8) _____ (think) of having the party at her parents' house in the country.
Sarah:	Is that the big house with the swimming pool?
Stephanie:	Yes, it is. Hopefully, we can ride her pony, too!
Sarah:	A birthday party with a clown and a pony! That (9) _____ (sound) like a great idea!
Stephanie:	Yes, I can't wait!

3 Complete the sentences with the past simple or the past continuous. Use the verbs in brackets.

1 India _____became_____ independent on 15th August 1947. (become)

2 I _____ the review, _____ the tickets and _____ the film. (read, buy, see)

3 As the athlete _____ the finish line, he collapsed. (cross)

4 In 2005, Fernando Alonso _____ his first Formula 1 title. (win)

5 While Laurie _____ the thriller, he _____ a loud noise. (watch, hear)

6 Isabel _____ the dog while her sister _____ . (walk, jog)

7 The guitarist _____ his story to the journalist. (sell)

8 The dog _____ a huge hole in the garden when Dad _____ him! (dig, not watch)

9 Our teacher _____ us a leaflet about Drummond Castle and _____ us to read it quietly. (give, ask)

10 Lynn _____ photos of the palace when she suddenly _____ ill. (take, feel)

4 Complete the magazine article with the past simple or the past continuous. Use the verbs in brackets.

> **Jennifer Aniston in brief**
>
> Jennifer Aniston (1) _____grew up_____ (grow up) in New York, and she (2) _____ (start) her acting career at the age of 11 when she (3) _____ (join) her school's drama club. While she (4) _____ (study) at school, she (5) _____ (become) interested in many forms of art. She (6) _____ (be) a talented painter, but acting also (7) _____ (appeal) to her. After graduating, acting became her primary focus.
>
> After a few minor roles, Aniston (8) _____ (consider) giving up acting, but her plans (9) _____ (change) in 1994 when a part in the series *Friends* (10) _____ (come) along. *Friends* became a worldwide success, and so did she!

5 Circle the correct words.

1 **You would use / Did you use to use** a dictionary for your French homework?

2 We **would listen / didn't use listen** to classical music when we were younger.

3 **Did the secretary use / Would the secretary** arrive at the office on time?

4 He **would be / used to be** a popular fashion designer.

5 I **would / didn't use to like** olives on my pizza.

6 Felicity **would / didn't use** dream of fame and fortune.

7 My grandmother **used to / would** live on a farm when she was younger.

8 We **used to / wouldn't** walk to school as we lived nearby.

6 Rewrite the second sentences using the correct form of *used to* or *get used to* so the meaning is similar to the first sentences.

1 The singer is starting to feel more comfortable about performing live.

The singer _____is getting used_____ to performing live.

2 I didn't enter competitions when I was young, but now I do.

I _____ enter competitions.

3 Sooner or later, our new neighbourhood won't feel so unusual.

Sooner or later, we will _____ our new neighbourhood.

4 Paying a lot of money for clothes is something new for us.

We _____ paying a lot of money for clothes.

5 Does Sandra feel odd working such long hours?

Is Sandra _____ working such long hours?

6 I soon learnt to speak French when I lived in Paris.

I _____ speaking French when I lived in Paris.

7 **The words in bold are wrong. Write the correct words.**

1   Jane **being** used to life as a celebrity.   _____is_____

2   Eric **would** like science, but now he hates it!   _____

3   These days, I am used to **be** interviewed by the press.   _____

4   In ancient times, people used to **travelling** on foot.   _____

5   Are you finally **being** used to catching the underground to Trafalgar Square?   _____

6   The Olympic Games used to **taking** place in Greece.   _____

WRITING PROJECT

8   **Look at this writing project about Rome. Circle the correct words.**

Rome

Rome (1) **is boasting / boasts** a history of more than 2,500 years. People (2) **believe / are believing** that Romulus founded Rome on 21st April, 753 BCE, and there is proof that people (3) **are used to living / used to live** there 14,000 years ago. Rome was a monarchy, a republic and then an empire, which (4) **was used to / used to** dominate most of Europe. The Roman Emperors (5) **were used to winning / are getting used to winning** their battles. However, the Muslim Arabs tried many times to conquer Rome, and eventually the Romans (6) **lost / lose**.

Rome (7) **was always being / was always** an important city throughout the Middle Ages and the Renaissance. In 1871, it (8) **was becoming / became** the capital of modern Italy.

Rome is full of monuments, parks and fountains. Sites (9) **are including / include** the Trevi fountain and the magnificent Colosseum. Here, in ancient times, citizens (10) **are used to watching / would watch** gladiators fighting. Now, the Colosseum (11) **receives / is receiving** approximately four million tourists per year.

Rome certainly (12) **is / is being** the Eternal City.

9   **Now it's your turn to do a project about a famous historical city. Find or draw a picture of this city and write about it.**

1 **Read.**

Tom has just won a gold medal! He's been training for this competition for years.

Present perfect simple

We use the **present perfect simple** to talk about something that
- started in the past but hasn't finished.
  We've been members of this club for six years.
- has just finished.
  Sam has just finished the poster.
- happened in the past, but we don't know or we don't say exactly when.
  Kelly has won three silver medals.
- happened in the past but that affects the present.
  I've broken my arm so I can't come skiing.

See the list of past participles on page 159.

Time expressions
We use the following **time expressions** with the **present perfect simple: already, ever, for, just, never, since, still, yet.**
We have known each other since 2004.
Philip has already started the project.

Remember!

We use **have been** when someone went somewhere and has returned.
My parents and I **have been** to Disneyland.
We use **have gone** when someone went somewhere and hasn't returned yet.
Natalie isn't at school. She**'s gone** home.

Affirmative	Negative	Question	Short answers	
I've become	I haven't become	Have I become ...?	Yes, I have.	No, I haven't.
you've become	you haven't become	Have you become ...?	Yes, you have.	No, you haven't.
he's become	he hasn't become	Has he become ...?	Yes, he has.	No, he hasn't.
she's become	she hasn't become	Has she become ...?	Yes, she has.	No, she hasn't.
it's become	it hasn't become	Has it become ...?	Yes, it has.	No, it hasn't.
we've become	we haven't become	Have we become ...?	Yes, we have.	No, we haven't.
you've become	you haven't become	Have you become ...?	Yes, you have.	No, you haven't.
they've become	they haven't become	Have they become ...?	Yes, they have.	No, they haven't.

2 Complete the sentences with the present perfect simple. Use the verbs in brackets.

1 My classmates and I ___have taken part___ in the kayaking race three times. (take part)

2 We _____ at this restaurant before. (not eat)

3 The weather forecaster _____ just _____ rain for tomorrow morning. (forecast)

4 Steve _____ the darts competition twice this year. (win)

5 _____ to a concert? (you ever / be)

6 I _____ my scuba diving instructor for five years. (know)

Present perfect continuous

We use the **present perfect continuous** to talk about
- something that started in the past and is still in progress.
  *Mum and Dad **have been cleaning** the house all day.*
- something that started in the past and has happened repeatedly.
  *The team **has been training** for the championship every day this week.*
- something that happened in the past and may have finished, but it has a result in the present.
  *The girls **have been studying** all night. They're exhausted.*
- how long something has been happening from the past up to now.
  *This athlete **has been competing** professionally for eight years.*

Remember!

We use **for** and **since** to show the duration of an action.
We've been living in this city **since** July.
Josh has been watching TV **for** two hours.

Time expressions
We use the following **time expressions** with the **present perfect continuous:**
all day, for a long time, for (very) long, years, lately, recently, since, for.
*He has been reading the newspaper **all morning**.*
*I haven't been living here **for very long**.*

Affirmative	Negative	Question	Short answers	
I've been running	I haven't been running	Have I been running ...?	Yes, I have.	No, I haven't.
you've been running	you haven't been running	Have you been running ...?	Yes, you have.	No, you haven't.
he's been running	he hasn't been running	Has he been running ...?	Yes, he has.	No, he hasn't.
she's been running	she hasn't been running	Has she been running ...?	Yes, she has.	No, she hasn't.
it's been running	it hasn't been running	Has it been running ...?	Yes, it has.	No, it hasn't.
we've been running	we haven't been running	Have we been running ...?	Yes, we have.	No, we haven't.
you've been running	you haven't been running	Have you been running ...?	Yes, you have.	No, you haven't.
they've been running	they haven't been running	Have they been running ...?	Yes, they have.	No, they haven't.

3 Complete the sentences with the present perfect continuous. Use these words.

make   not learn   perform   ~~play~~   practise   write

1 Daniel ___has been playing___ chess for six years.

2 _____ you _____ your own blog since last month?

3 The children _____ a lot of progress at school this year.

4 Sebastian _____ English for very long.

5 _____ you _____ with the tennis champion?

6 Julie is a wonderful musician. She _____ since she was 18.

Present perfect simple vs present perfect continuous

We use the **present perfect simple** to talk about something we have done or achieved. The action is complete.
*My classmates and I **have finished** our history project.*

But we use the **present perfect continuous** to talk about an action that has duration. It doesn't matter if the action has finished or not.
*My little sister **has been playing** all afternoon.*

We also use the **present perfect simple** to talk about how many times an action has happened and to answer the questions **How much ...?, How many ...?** and **How many times ...?**
***How many times** have you visited Madrid?*
*We**'ve visited** Madrid three times.*

But we use the **present perfect continuous** to answer the question **How long ...?**
***How long** has Jason been waiting?*
*He **has been waiting** for half an hour.*

4 **Circle the correct words.**

1 The toy company **has constructed / has been constructing** model planes for many years.

2 Sam **hasn't played / hasn't been playing** on the basketball team for long.

3 How long **have you done / have you been doing** karate classes?

4 Our coach **has shouted / has been shouting** all morning!

5 The volunteers **have sold / have been selling** tickets since last Monday.

6 How many seashells **have you collected / have you been collecting**?

5 **Complete the questions with the present perfect simple or the present perfect continuous using the words in brackets. Then write short answers.**

1 _____Have you found_____ the tickets for the concert yet? (you / find) ✓   _____Yes, I have._____

2 _____ to fix this remote control all afternoon? (Harry / try) ✗   _____

3 _____ since eleven o'clock this morning? (they / wait) ✓   _____

4 _____ their model planes for long? (the children / fly) ✗   _____

5 _____ her studies? (your sister / finish) ✗   _____

6 _____ all her milk? (the baby / drink) ✓   _____

6 **Rewrite the sentences using the words given. Use between two and five words.**

1 I met Sarah six years ago and we are still friends.
I _____have known Sarah for_____ six years. **known**

2 We started jogging three hours ago and we are still jogging.
We _____ three hours. **been**

3 Tommy scored three goals and the match isn't over.
Tommy _____ three times so far in the match. **has**

4 My parents visited Rome in 2007, 2009 and 2017.
My parents _____ three times. **visited**

5 You started sailing at six o'clock this morning and you are still on the lake!
_____ since six o'clock this morning. **have**

6 Sandra used to collect posters, but she doesn't any more.
Sandra _____ posters recently. **been**

7 Complete the telephone conversation with the present perfect simple or the present perfect continuous. Use the words in brackets.

Millie: Joe, I can't talk now. I've got to get ready for my rounders match.

Joe: Rounders? What's that?

Millie: (1) _Haven't you heard_ (you / not hear) of rounders? It's a sport. School children (2) _____ (play) it since the 15th century and it (3) _____ (always be) especially popular with girls.

Joe: Oh, I see. What do you have to do?

Millie: Well, you have to hit a small hard ball with a bat and then run round the pitch.

Joe: It sounds like baseball.

Millie: Yes, it's also similar to cricket. For years, schools (4) _____ (hold) competitions. It's fun.

Joe: Mm. I (5) _____ (never be) keen on cricket, or baseball. They're too boring for me.

Millie: Well, my team (6) _____ (practise) for weeks now. The big match is today and we (7) _____ (never beat) our rivals.

Joe: Good luck then!

Millie: Thanks!

8 Say it! Imagine that you have arranged a surprise party for a friend. Talk with your partner about what preparations have been made. Use the present perfect simple, the present perfect continuous and these suggestions to help you.

- order a cake
- decorate the room
- lay out the food
- arrange tables and chairs
- select music

I have bought the soft drinks.

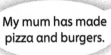

My mum has made pizza and burgers.

1   Read.

Relative clauses

We use **relative clauses** to give more information about people, animals, places and things. A **relative clause** begins with a **relative pronoun** (**who, whom, which, whose**) or a **relative adverb** (**when, where, why**).
We use

- **who** for people.
  *There's the runner **who** broke the world record.*
- **whom** for people.
  *They chose the builder **whom** I had recommended.*
- **whose** to say that something belongs to someone.
  *There's the boy **whose** bike was stolen.*
- **which** for animals and things.
  *Where's the skirt **which** I bought in the sales?*
- **where** for places.
  *That's the store **where** I buy my shoes.*
- **when** for the time something happens.
  *Do you remember the day **when** we got lost?*
- **why** for the reason something happened.
  *Do you know the reason **why** Jane is ignoring me?*

We can use **whom** for people when the relative pronoun refers to the object of the sentence. However, it isn't usually used in everyday speech.

*The diving instructor **whom** I spoke to was very friendly.*
*The diving instructor (**that/who**) I spoke to was very friendly.*

When there is a preposition before the relative pronoun, we must use **whom** and not **who**.
*The diving instructor **to whom** I spoke was very friendly.*

A relative adverb can be used instead of a preposition and a relative pronoun.
When can replace **in/on which**
Where can replace **in/at which**
Why can replace **for which**
*December is the month **in which** he celebrates his birthday.*
*December is the month **when** he celebrates his birthday.*

2 Complete the sentences with *who*, *whom*, *which*, *whose*, *where*, *when* or *why*.

1 There's the guide _____ who _____ speaks many languages.

2 Do you remember the gymnast _____ tricks were very dangerous?

3 Is Lucy the girl to _____ you tell your secrets?

4 Name the river _____ flows through central London.

5 My cousin doesn't remember the year _____ she went to London.

6 I don't understand the reason _____ people enjoy extreme sports.

7 We participate in activities _____ are for adventurous types.

8 Can we visit the national park _____ we saw the huge waterfall?

Defining relative clauses

Defining relative clauses give essential information about a person, animal, place or thing that we are referring to. Without this information, the sentence doesn't make sense. We don't use commas in **defining relative clauses**.
*There's the player **who** scored the goal.*
*I visited the school **where** my mum used to go.*

In a **defining relative clause**, we can use **that** instead of **who** or **which**.
*The student **who/that** won the scholarship is my cousin.*
*The dog **which/that** ran onto the tennis court was Nancy's.*

We don't need to use a **relative pronoun** (**who**, **which** or **that**) when it refers to the object of the **defining relative clause**.
*Jonathan is the boy **who** they chose as captain of the baseball team.*
Jonathan is the boy they chose as captain of the baseball team.

3 Circle the correct words.

1 The hobby **which** / **who** I took up wasn't very interesting.

2 Is that the sports centre **where** / **which** you go bowling?

3 The sports car **who** / **–** I like is very expensive.

4 Let's go to the pool **which** / **where** I go diving.

5 Show me the girl **who** / **whose** father is a film star.

6 I can't remember the day **when** / **where** we went to the beach.

7 The song **when** / **that** won the competition is great.

8 Tell me the reason **why** / **which** you don't want to come to my party.

Non-defining relative clauses

Non-defining relative clauses give extra information about the person, animal, place or thing that we are referring to. This information isn't necessary for the sentence to make sense and it is separated from the rest of the sentence with commas.
*The new adventure park, **which** has many exciting rides, is very close to my house.*
*The track and field athlete, **who** won the 100-metre race, is visiting our school next week.*

In a **non-defining relative clause**, we can't use **that** instead of **who** or **which**.

We can't omit the **relative pronoun** (**who**, **which** or **whose**) in a **non-defining relative clause**, even if it refers to the object of the **relative clause**.

4 Underline the non-defining relative clauses and circle the defining relative clauses.

1 There's the girl who told me about the new rules.

2 The famous singer, who has received three gold records, is signing autographs.

3 The naughty twins, whose parents are forever shouting, have just broken their neighbour's window.

4 Can you help the children who are having difficulty with English?

5 The golf club, at which Mum and Dad play golf with their friends, has many famous members.

6 Paris is the place where the 2024 Olympic Games will take place.

5 Combine the sentences using the words in bold.

1 Max is a great tennis player. He has won many trophies. **who**

   Max, who has won many trophies, is a great tennis player.

2 Anna plays in an orchestra. She is my next-door neighbour. **who**

   _____

3 My uncle Robert drives a sports car. His favourite pastime is racing. **whose**

   _____

4 The 2012 Olympic Games took place in London. They were a great success. **which**

   _____

5 Timothy is my cousin. I give him all my old clothes. **whom**

   _____

6 Notting Hill is an area in London. The film *Notting Hill* was shot there. **where**

   _____

6 Cross out *that, which* or *who* where possible.

1 Is that the gorge that Peter was telling us about?

2 Those children, who are white water rafting, are very reckless.

3 The play which we saw last night was so boring!

4 There's the rucksack that I've been looking for!

5 I interviewed the writer that had won the Nobel Prize in Literature.

6 I often read books which are about health and fitness.

7 Complete the text. Use these words.

> when   where   which   who   whose   why

1966 was the year (1) _____ when _____ England won the World Cup. On the day of the final, 98,000 people arrived at Wembley Stadium, (2) _____ the match took place. Germany was the team (3) _____ England had to play against.

The first player to celebrate was Helmut Haller, (4) _____ scored the first goal for Germany. The English fans cheered for Martin Peters, (5) _____ goal put England back in the match a little later.

A 2–2 draw at the end of 90 minutes was the reason (6) _____ the match went into extra time. In the 98th minute, Geoff Hurst scored a goal, although many people thought the ball didn't cross the line. He scored again in the last minute, so England finally won the World Cup Final 4–2.

8 Rewrite the sentences using the words given. Use between two and five words.

1 Dina doesn't like risky sports. That's why she doesn't try mountain climbing. **for**

The reason ___for which Dina doesn't___ try mountain climbing is that she doesn't like risky sports.

2 My teammates and I played handball in a stadium yesterday. The Olympic Games had taken place there. **where**

My teammates and I played handball in a stadium _____ taken place.

3 Do you know the actor? They presented an award to him. **whom**

Do you know the actor to _____ an award?

4 Jessica Ennis won the Olympic heptathlon in 2012. I remember that day! **when**

I remember the _____ Jessica Ennis won the Olympic heptathlon.

5 Ginnie recognised the man. His picture appeared in the newspaper. **whose**

Ginnie recognised the man _____ in the newspaper.

6 Kite surfing is my favourite sport. It isn't very common. **which**

Kite surfing, _____ , isn't very common.

7 The couple got married in the hotel. They had first met there. **where**

The couple got married in the hotel _____ first met.

8 Emma is my best friend. She is a talented artist. **who**

Emma, _____ , is a talented artist.

9 Say it! Talk to your partner about these things using defining and non-defining clauses.

- a person you know well
- your favourite hobby
- the time you had a lot of fun
- some information about your mum's car
- a food you dislike
- a place you and your friends go to regularly

Tennis is the sport that I really enjoy.

Paul, who is my best friend, lives next door to our school.

1 **Read.**

I'm afraid you're too late for your flight. You'll have to buy a ticket for the next flight.

This is so unfair. I don't have enough money to buy a new ticket.

Too and enough

We use **too + adjective** to show that there is more of something than we need or want.
*Cricket is **too boring** for me.*

We use **adjective + enough** to show that there is as much of something as we need.
*Pat is **experienced enough** for the job.*

We can also use **enough** before uncountable nouns and plural countable nouns to show that there is as much or as many of something as we need.
*There is **enough cheese** to make a sandwich.*
*There are **enough contestants** for the art competition.*

We use **not enough** when there is less of something than we need or want.
There aren't enough glasses for everyone.
We haven't got enough money for an indoor swimming pool.

2 **Complete the sentences with *too* or *enough*.**

1 I'm not keen on bungee jumping, as I'm not adventurous _____ *enough* _____ .

2 We don't want to go out. We're _____ tired.

3 Have you got _____ players for the Cup Final?

4 Rosie doesn't have _____ time to take up a new sport.

5 Yoga is _____ boring for me!

6 Is Jamie fit _____ to take part in the marathon?

7 Charlie doesn't want skiing lessons. He thinks it's _____ hard.

8 I don't have _____ money to buy new trainers.

3 Complete the dialogue. Use these phrases.

> enough time   ~~not talented enough~~   not tall enough
> not too late   too much homework   too strenuous

Stephen: Do you think Robbie will become a professional tennis player?

Alicia: I don't know. In my opinion, he's (1) _____ not talented enough _____ to make it to the top.

Stephen: Really? He's always playing in tournaments though. I admire him. I haven't got
(2) _____ to play in tournaments. We always have
(3) _____ .

Alicia: I know. It's not easy training every day.

Stephen: And tennis is (4) _____
for me. I prefer water sports.

Alicia: What would you like to become, Stephen?

Stephen: I've always wanted to surf, but I've never had time to take it up.

Alicia: Well, it's (5) _____ now. You're only 14!

Stephen: Mm, you're right. Oh, I like basketball, too.

Alicia: Sorry, Stephen, you're just (6) _____ !
Basketball players are twice your height!

4 Choose the correct answers.

1 I haven't got _____ to do a project on wildlife.
  a too much information
  b enough information ✓
  c not enough information

2 We can walk to the youth club. It's _____ .
  a too far
  b far enough
  c close enough

3 People _____ these days.
  a don't have enough free time
  b enough free time
  c don't have free time too

4 Parachuting is much _____ . I'm not going to try it.
  a safe enough
  b too dangerous
  c dangerous enough

5 You won't be able to ski today. There _____
  on the mountains.
  a isn't enough snow
  b too much snow
  c is enough snow

6 You're so tall now. Your trousers _____ for you.
  a are long enough
  b aren't too long
  c aren't long enough

7 Oliver wants to keep fit, but he _____ to join a gym.
  a isn't old enough
  b isn't too old
  c isn't enough old

8 Just be patient! There _____ balloons for everyone.
  a too much
  b are enough
  c not enough

9 There are _____ people in front of me. I can't see who's winning the race!
  a aren't enough
  b enough
  c too many

10 There won't be a party at the end of the year. Unfortunately, parents _____ to help.
  a aren't willing enough
  b too willing
  c are enough willing

5 Look at the pictures and complete the sentences with *too* or *enough* and these words.

| expense | few | little | quiet | ~~warm~~ | young |

1 It isn't _____warm enough_____ to jump in the pool.

2 There are _____ ice creams for the children.

3 Summer camp is _____ this year. We're not going to go.

4 It isn't _____ for Mr Wilson to work.

5 Sammy is _____ to take part in the archery competition.

6 There's _____ sugar to make a cake.

6 Say it! Imagine your seven-year-old brother wants to take up windsurfing and you think that he shouldn't. Talk with your partner about what you would tell him. Use *too*, *enough* and these suggestions to help you.

- dangerous
- tiring
- risky
- strenuous

> I don't think you are old enough to take up windsurfing.

> I think it's too strenuous for you.

1 Read.

Why is Julia so upset?

She had been waiting for her dad to arrive, but he had to work late.

Past perfect continuous

We use the **past perfect continuous** to
- emphasise the duration of an action that was in progress before another action or time in the past.
  *I **had been waiting** for Jane for half an hour before she finally arrived.*
- talk about an action that was in progress in the past which affected a later action or state.
  *Our neighbours **had been making** a lot of noise, so we finally called the police.*

We form the affirmative with **had been** and the main verb with the ending **–ing**.
*Jennifer **had been shopping** for hours before she went home.*

In the negative form we use **hadn't been** and the main verb with the ending **–ing**.
*Paul **hadn't been working** for very long when he got a promotion.*

In the question form we use **had been** and the main verb with the ending **–ing**. In short answers we only use **had**. We don't use the main verb.
***Had** you **been watching** TV all evening before you went to bed?*
*Yes, I **had**.*

Time expressions
We use the following **time expressions** with the **past perfect continuous: all day, for weeks/ ages/a (very) long time, since four o'clock, at the time.**

Affirmative	Negative	Question	Short answers	
I had been waiting	I hadn't been waiting	Had I been waiting ...?	Yes, I had.	No, I hadn't.
you had been waiting	you hadn't been waiting	Had you been waiting ...?	Yes, you had.	No, you hadn't.
he had been waiting	he hadn't been waiting	Had he been waiting ...?	Yes, he had.	No, he hadn't.
she had been waiting	she hadn't been waiting	Had she been waiting ...?	Yes, she had.	No, she hadn't.
it had been waiting	it hadn't been waiting	Had it been waiting ...?	Yes, it had.	No, it hadn't.
we had been waiting	we hadn't been waiting	Had we been waiting ...?	Yes, we had.	No, we hadn't.
you had been waiting	you hadn't been waiting	Had you been waiting ...?	Yes, you had.	No, you hadn't.
they had been waiting	they hadn't been waiting	Had they been waiting ...?	Yes, they had.	No, they hadn't.

2 Complete the sentences with the past perfect continuous. Use the verbs in brackets.

1 Billy _____had been working_____ on a farm before he moved to the city. (work)

2 Marcia _____ all night before she saw the lights of the city. (drive)

3 I _____ on the rooftop for very long when it started to rain! (not sit)

4 We _____ the hospital for two hours before the ambulance finally arrived. (phone)

5 Tim and Wendy _____ tennis for long when Wendy hurt her leg. (not play)

6 Our teacher _____ about the pros and cons of exams all morning when suddenly there was a power cut. (talk)

3 Look at the pictures and complete the sentences with the correct form of the past perfect continuous. Use these verbs.

> argue   not talk   ~~not wait~~   rely   show   study

1 Grandma ___hadn't been waiting___ for a long time when the bus arrived.

4 Mum _____ me how to use my new mobile phone just before Dad came home.

2 The girls _____ about what colour to paint their room before they agreed to paint it yellow.

5 Gemma fell asleep during the test because she _____ all night!

3 Joe _____ on his parents to drive him everywhere before he passed his driving test.

6 Kerry and Lily finally made up. They _____ for weeks!

4 Complete the questions with the past perfect continuous and the words in brackets. Then complete the short answers.

1 ___Had you been walking___ the dog before I arrived? (you / walk)

Yes, ___I had___ .

2 _____ in an office before he became a teacher? (Jack / work)

No, _____ .

3 _____ in the fields when she found the stray cat? (Teresa / cycle)

Yes, _____ .

4 _____ at Newcastle University before you moved to Manchester? (you / study)

No, _____ .

5 _____ for a long time before she opened the door? (Clare's classmates / knock)

Yes, _____ .

5 Complete the dialogue with the past perfect continuous. Use the verbs in brackets.

Freddie: How was your summer in New York?

Alice: Good.

Freddie: Good? You (1) ___'d/had been talking___ (talk) about it day and night before you left!

Alice: I know. The truth is, I (2) _____ (look forward to) it for ages. I (3) _____ (not think) about anything else.

Freddie: I remember! And for a very long time, your cousin Trish (4) _____ (boast) about how big her college was and how great life was in New York.

Alice: Mm.

Freddie: So, isn't life great in The Big Apple?

Alice: Well, it is. New York is amazing. It's absolutely beautiful, with many historic sites, museums and beautiful parks. I (5) _____ (dream) of walking through Central Park for years!

Freddie: So?

Alice: It made me realise how lucky we are to live in the countryside.

Freddie: I know. Trish doesn't think so though, does she? Before she went to the States, she (6) _____ (complain) about how dull country life is.

Alice: You're right! Trish loves it there.

I love New York

6 Say it! Look at these pictures with your partner. Talk about what the children had been doing when the storm struck.

> Some boys had been playing football when the storm struck.

> These girls had been playing tennis when the storm struck.

1 **Read.**

We had been cleaning the house for three hours before our cousins arrived.

Past perfect simple

We use the **past perfect simple** to talk about
- something that happened in the past before another action in the past.
  *I **had set** the security alarm before I left home.*
- something that happened before a specific time in the past. We often use the word **by** to mean before or not later than.
  *By ten o'clock yesterday morning, we **had done** our shopping.*
- something that happened in the past and had an effect on a later action.
  *Julie **had won** a lot of money so she decided to buy an apartment in the city centre.*

See the list of past participles on page 159.

Time expressions
We use the following **time expressions** with the **past perfect simple: after, already, as soon as, before, by (time or date), just, when.**
*Janet had **just** sat down when the phone rang.*
*Brian had **already** handed in his assignment.*

Affirmative	Negative	Question	Short answers	
I had found	I hadn't found	Had I found ...?	Yes, I had.	No, I hadn't.
you had found	you hadn't found	Had you found ...?	Yes, you had.	No, you hadn't.
he had found	he hadn't found	Had he found ...?	Yes, he had.	No, he hadn't.
she had found	she hadn't found	Had she found ...?	Yes, she had.	No, she hadn't.
it had found	it hadn't found	Had it found ...?	Yes, it had.	No, it hadn't.
we had found	we hadn't found	Had we found ...?	Yes, we had.	No, we hadn't.
you had found	you hadn't found	Had you found ...?	Yes, you had.	No, you hadn't.
they had found	they hadn't found	Had they found ...?	Yes, they had.	No, they hadn't.

2 Complete the sentences with the past perfect simple. Use the verbs in brackets.

1   When I arrived home, I realised I ____'d/had forgotten____ my bag on the bus. (forget)

2   Mandy felt terrible because she _____ all night. (not sleep)

3   I only understood the film because I _____ the book. (read)

4   As soon as I _____ the room, my mum called me back. (leave)

5   Sebastian _____ the car when it started to rain. (just wash)

6   Tim _____ the question until Mr Jones explained it to him. (not understand)

3 Write questions.

1   _Had you fallen asleep by ten o'clock last night?_____

Yes, I had fallen asleep by ten o'clock last night.

2   _____

No, Christine hadn't stayed on a farm before.

3   _____

Yes, our grandparents had lived in Ireland before we were born.

4   _____

No, they hadn't eaten all the ice cream before I arrived.

5   _____

Yes, I had just moved house when I met Sue.

6   _____

Yes, I had already replied to his email.

Past perfect simple vs past perfect continuous

We use both the **past perfect simple** and **past perfect continuous** to talk about actions that happened in the past before another past action.
*Natalie **had finished** her project before she went out.*
*We **had been waiting** for ages before the doctor arrived.*

However, we use the **past perfect continuous** to emphasise how long the first action was in progress for.
*My classmates and I **had been raising** money for stray animals for a very long time.*

We also use the **past perfect continuous** to show that we don't know whether the action was completed or not.
*Jason **had been exercising**, so he was tired.*

4 Circle the correct words.

1   Before we moved to the city, my family and I **had always liked** / had always been liking living in the suburbs.

2   I **had studied / had been studying** at the library all morning when I decided to take a break.

3   My classmates and I **hadn't noticed / hadn't been noticing** the adventure playground before Dad showed it to us.

4   Before I joined the local gym, I **hadn't realised / hadn't been realising** how important exercise is.

5   The children were exhausted because they **had swum / had been swimming** all afternoon.

6   The dog **had dug / had been digging** all morning before it finally found its bone.

5 Look at the pictures and complete the sentences with the correct form of the past perfect simple or the past perfect continuous. Use these verbs.

~~depart~~   do   do   miss   not leave   train

1   When Tom got to the station the train __had departed__ .

2   Mandy realised how much she _____ the peace and quiet of the countryside.

3   Dad was very tired at lunch. He _____ the gardening all morning.

4   Josh was angry as his little brother _____ him any biscuits.

5   Marcus was exhausted because he _____ all morning.

6   The children _____ the experiment before they wrote the report.

6 Complete the diary entry with the past perfect simple or the past perfect continuous. Use the verbs in brackets.

Last week, my cousin Oscar, who lives in a village, came to stay with me for the weekend. I (1) _d/had been wondering_ (wonder) where to take him for hours when Oscar suggested going to the zoo. I (2) _____ (never be) keen on zoos, but Oscar (3) _____ (not visit) a zoo before, so we decided to go.

After we (4) _____ (travel) on the bus for an hour, we arrived at the zoo. There are many animals and exotic birds, and I was surprised because I (5) _____ (realise) how big the park was.

After Oscar and I (6) _____ (walk) around for hours, we decided to sit down and have a drink at the café. It was very peaceful and relaxing. Later, we continued walking and we saw some beautiful lions, tigers, zebras, bears and a giraffe. Oscar (7) _____ (not see) a giraffe before and he was thrilled!

I (8) _____ (never want) to visit a zoo, but I really enjoyed this experience.

7 Say it! Tom had lots of things to do before he went on holiday. Look at his list below and talk to your partner about what he had and hadn't done before he left for the airport.

✓ pack suitcase
✗ water plants
✓ close all the windows
✗ wash the car
✗ tidy the living room
✓ exchange money
✓ buy new sunglasses
✓ ring Mum and Dad to say goodbye
✓ cancel newspaper

Tom had packed his suitcase before he left for the airport.

Tom hadn't watered the plants before he left for the airport.

1 **Read.**

This is an amazing view.

This is the most beautiful view I've ever seen.

The indefinite article

We use the **indefinite articles a/an**
- with a singular countable noun when we mention it for the first time.
  *This is **an** amazing adventure park.*
- with a singular countable noun when making a general statement.
  *You don't need **a** car in the city centre.*
- with nouns which refer to professions, nationalities or religions.
  *Mr Greenhalf is **a** French teacher.*
  *Philip is **an** American.*
- with certain numbers instead of **one**, and some quantifying phrases such as: **a thousand**, **twice a week**, **once an hour**, etc.
  *Mum drives to work **once a week**.*

We don't use the indefinite articles **a/an** with
- plural countable nouns or uncountable nouns.
  We always drink milk for breakfast.
- adjectives which aren't followed by a noun.
  My cousin is adventurous!
- the names of meals, unless there is an adjective before them.
  Can you come to my house for dinner?
  *Mum cooked **a** lovely meal last night.*

Remember!

When a word begins with a vowel, but the vowel sounds like a consonant in the word, we use **a**.
Jennifer is **a university** graduate.

When a word begins with a consonant, but the consonant sounds like a vowel in the word, we use **an**.
I want to buy **an MP4 player**.

2 **Complete the sentences with *a, an* or –.**

1 Catherine's dad is _____*an*_____ architect.

2 There's _____ great funfair just outside the city centre.

3 Our teacher is going to take us out for _____ lunch.

4 The flight to Paris is approximately _____ hour long.

5 Dad takes _____ sugar with his coffee.

6 I really need _____ new sofa for the living room.

7 We go skiing in the Swiss Alps once _____ year.

8 William wrote _____ interesting story.

The definite article

We use the **definite article the**
- with singular and plural countable and uncountable nouns to talk about something specific or when we mention something for a second time.
  *Can you pass me **the** salt, please?*
  *Mum bought me a T-shirt. **The** T-shirt is really cool.*
- before unique nouns, names of hotels, theatres and musical instruments.
  *We haven't seen **the** sun for three days because it's been raining!*
  *Are you staying at **the** Marriott Hotel?*
  *Salma plays **the** trumpet.*
- for historical periods or events.
  *At the moment, we're learning about **the** Middle Ages.*
- for groups of islands, mountain ranges, rivers and deserts.
  *We're renting a house on one of **the** Greek islands.*
  *Kate is doing a project on **the** Sahara Desert.*
- before superlatives.
  *This is **the** most beautiful view I've ever seen.*
- before nationalities.
  ***The** Spanish are keen on football.*
- with dates and with the words **morning, afternoon, evening** and **night**.
  *Amy was born on **the** 6th of November.*
- with adjectives referring to a group of people.
  *We really should help **the** homeless more.*

We don't use the **definite article** with
- proper nouns.
  James is a talented table tennis player.
- the names of sports, games, colours, days, months, holidays, subjects of study and languages (not followed by the word **language**).
  Kylie plays ice-hockey for the national team.
  *Luke speaks French. (But Luke speaks **the** French language.)*
- names of most countries (but *the USA, the Netherlands*), cities, streets (but *the High Street*), parks, bridges, islands, lakes and continents.
  Marcus was born in Beirut.
  We'll meet you at the café on Bond Street.
- with the words **school, hospital, prison, university** when they are used as a general term.
  Helen's been at university for two years.

3 Complete the sentences with *the* or –.

1 My grandparents moved to _____the_____ United States after _____the_____ Second World War.

2 Every year, Elisa travels to _____ Sweden.

3 _____ Saturday is my favourite day of the week.

4 Is _____ head teacher at your school Australian?

5 This is _____ most spectacular concert I've ever been to!

6 We went on a boat trip along _____ River Nile.

7 Many people can speak _____ English language.

8 I used to love playing _____ hide-and-seek.

4 Complete the text with *a, an, the* or –.

Mount Snowdon is (1) _____the_____ highest mountain in Wales and one of (2) _____ highest mountains in (3) _____ Great Britain. It is located in (4) _____ national park and is about 250 miles away from (5) _____ Cardiff, (6) _____ Wales' capital city.

In the past, (7) _____ only way to the top was on foot. Nowadays, there is (8) _____ railway. Thousands of people climb (9) _____ mountain every year to enjoy (10) _____ amazing view.

5 **Circle the correct words.**

1 We're going backpacking around **Greek Islands** /**the Greek Islands** this summer.

2 Have you ever seen **an eagle / eagle**?

3 At the moment, we are learning about **the Battle of Trafalgar / Battle of Trafalgar** in history.

4 We have raised a large amount of money to help **the poor / poor**.

5 We had **a beautiful breakfast / beautiful breakfast** on the roof garden.

6 The new play is on at **Orion Theatre / the Orion Theatre**.

6 **The words in bold are wrong. Write – or the correct words.**

1 Let's go to **a** new shopping mall this afternoon. It's just opened! _____the_____

2 These are **a** worst living conditions I have ever seen. _____

3 My parents and I are travelling to **the** Sharm El-Sheikh this summer. _____

4 Can you come to our country house for **the** lunch next Saturday? _____

5 This is **the** very nice violin. _____

6 Harry graduated from university and he became **the** lawyer. _____

7 **Say it! Talk to your partner about what you know about these places.**

Everest

The River Nile

Adventure Park

Paris

New York

Petra

Library

The Alps

The Zoo

Mount Everest is the tallest mountain in the world.

Paris is a city in France.

Review

1 Complete the sentences with the present perfect simple. Use these verbs.

> be   buy   give   not finish   take part   ~~visit~~

1 I _____'ve/have_____ never _____visited_____ such a picturesque village before!
2 My classmates and I _____ in three competitions this year.
3 I _____ my homework yet.
4 My grandparents _____ just _____ a new apartment near the botanical gardens.
5 You _____ in the adventure park since eleven o'clock this morning! Aren't you tired?
6 The government _____ our local community some money for bicycle lanes.

2 Complete this text with the present perfect continuous. Use the verbs in brackets.

My family and I (1) ___have been looking for___ (look for) a cottage in Devon, but they all seem to be very expensive. We chose Devon because we (2) _____ (spend) our weekends there for years now.

We all like peaceful weekends away from the hustle and bustle of the city centre. Dad and Joe, my brother, enjoy walking, and for the past three years, they (3) _____ (trek) with a group of people from the area. We (4) _____ (argue) about where to buy this cottage, as Dad, Mum and Joe want to be near the hills, but my sister and I (5) _____ (hope) to find a house nearer to the sea. We enjoy swimming and water sports. My sister (6) _____ (dive) since she was very young and I (7) _____ (sail) for two years.

At the moment, we can't find anything, so we (8) _____ (stay) in a little hotel. I hope we find something soon.

3 Complete the dialogue with the present perfect simple or the present perfect continuous. Use the verbs in brackets.

Rosie: Billy, I think we (1) _____'ve/have_____ finally _____found_____ (find) a solution for homeless people in our community.

Billy: Really? That's great. We (2) _____ (try) for so long!

Rosie: I spoke to the mayor and he (3) _____ (agree) to provide money for a shelter. He also wants to encourage residents to raise money for homeless people.

Billy: We (4) _____ (disagree) about this issue for the past year. Why (5) _____ he suddenly _____ (decide) to help?

Rosie: For a very long time, many people (6) _____ (complain) about the number of people living on the streets. I think he (7) _____ finally _____ (realise) how serious the problem is. We're meeting later on to discuss how to raise the money.

Billy: I'll come, too. We (8) _____ (worry) about this problem for ages!

4 The words in bold are wrong. Write the correct words.

1 This house, **where** has got a rooftop garden, is extremely expensive. _____which_____
2 That's the girl **whom** won the scholarship to study abroad. _____
3 The botanical garden, **which** there is a huge variety of tropical plants, is on the outskirts of the city. _____
4 Can you please tell me the time **which** the library opens? _____
5 I know the lady **that** son owns a pet tarantula. _____
6 The sports centre, in **where** there'll be many new facilities, should open by the end of the year. _____

5 Choose the correct answers.

1 Sam is _____ to go to the sports centre.
  a enough tired
  (b) too tired
  c tired enough

2 I'm not keen on the inner city. It's just _____ for me.
  a noisy enough
  b too noisy
  c enough noisy

3 There aren't any big animals in the country park. It is _____ .
  a not large enough
  b too large
  c small enough

4 My neighbourhood is dull as there _____ .
  a aren't enough facilities
  b are too many facilities
  c are enough facilities

5 You'll easily get into the local university. You're _____ .
  a too clever
  b clever enough
  c not clever enough

6 This river is _____ to swim in. Let's go to the swimming pool.
  a polluted enough
  b enough polluted
  c too polluted

6 Complete the sentences with the past perfect continuous. Use the words in brackets.

1 Rosie and Clare ____had been talking____ during yesterday's lesson so they hadn't heard about today's test. (talk)

2 _____ for long when the coach arrived? (you / practise)

3 The local community _____ a new library before they ran out of money. (build)

4 We were exhausted last night. We _____ the gardening all afternoon. (do)

5 _____ for long before he found his way out of the maze? (Johnny / walk)

6 Mum _____ for long before Dad got home. (not cook)

7 Sarah _____ all day, so she was very tired. (study)

8 _____ for long when she finally arrived? (you / wait)

7 Circle the correct words.

1 Before last night, I **hadn't watched** / **hadn't been watching** a 3D film on TV.

2 We **had hiked** / **had been hiking** all morning when we finally saw a café.

3 **Had Mr Terry taught** / **Had Mr Terry been teaching** for years before he decided to retire?

4 Until I saw Max bungee jump off the bridge, I **had never wanted** / **had never been wanting** to try it myself.

5 Mrs Robinson **had never realised** / **had never been realising** how dull the programme was.

6 Harriet and James got home late. They **had sold** / **had been selling** tickets all evening.

7 Mum **had cleaned** / **had been cleaning** the house all day before the guests arrived.

8 I **had been seeing** / **had seen** that film before.

8 Complete the article with *a*, *an*, *the* or *–*.

PILATES

If you want to strengthen your muscles, Pilates is (1) ____a____ great idea. It is (2) _____ system of physical fitness, which has improved (3) _____ lives of people of all ages all over (4) _____ world.

People started practising (5) _____ Pilates in (6) _____ early twentieth century, when (7) _____ gymnast Joseph Pilates invented the system. His aim was to unite our body and mind, and therefore (8) _____ lot of concentration is required. (9) _____ basic aim of Pilates is to help you breathe properly and strengthen your muscles, making you feel healthier all round.

It really is worth (10) _____ try, so why not give it a go!

WRITING PROJECT

9 Look at a project about the Old Town of Heidelberg. Choose the correct answers.

The Old Town of Heidelberg

The Old Town or Altstadt of Heidelberg is located on the southern side of (1) _____ Neckar River. It is (2) _____ beautiful town and many visitors walk through the maze of cobbled streets and admire the historical architecture. For example, the city hall, which (3) _____ in its present form since 1701; the Haus zum Ritter, which is one of (4) _____ oldest buildings in Heidelberg; and the Ruprecht Karls University, which dates back to the late 14th century, to name just a few.

Visitors can follow (5) _____ Hauptstrasse, (6) _____ is the city's high street, all the way to the ruins of the famous Heidelberg Castle. They can also visit antique shops, art galleries, trendy boutiques and department stores. Or they can just enjoy the view sitting at one of the many cafés. The Café Knoesel was opened in 1863 and (7) _____ popular. It is famous for its delicious chocolate praline.

Locals and visitors alike can enjoy the various events that take place during the year, such as the Heidelberg Castle Festival, which has fascinating theatrical productions and open-air events, and the Heidelberg Autumn Fair, (8) _____ people can try local specialities.

1 **a** –   **b** a   **c** the
2 **a** –   **b** a   **c** the
3 **a** exists   **b** has existed   **c** had existed
4 **a** –   **b** a   **c** the
5 **a** –   **b** a   **c** the
6 **a** that   **b** where   **c** which
7 **a** will be **b** has always been **c** have always been
8 **a** that   **b** which   **c** where

10 Now it's your turn to do a project about a town. Find or draw a picture of the town and write about it.

1 **Read.**

Future simple

We use the **future simple**
- to talk about predictions.
  It'll be a long and tiring journey.
- to talk about decisions we make at the time of speaking.
  I'll go to the bakery and buy some bread.
- to make offers, promises, threats or warnings.
  You must be hungry. I'll make you a sandwich.
- to ask someone to do something for us.
  Will you call Jane for me, please?
- to talk about opinions for the future usually after
  think, hope, be sure, believe, bet and **probably**.
  *I'm **sure** Brian **will pass** with flying colours.*

Note: We use **shall** with **I** or **we** in questions when we want to offer to do something or suggest something.
Shall I make you a milkshake?

Time expressions
We use the following **time expressions** with the **future simple: tomorrow, in the morning/afternoon/evening, this week/weekend/month/year, in a week/month/year,** etc.
I'll take the dog for a walk in the afternoon.

Affirmative	Negative	Question	Short answers	
I'll help	I won't help	Will I help ...?	Yes, I will.	No, I won't.
you'll help	you won't help	Will you help ...?	Yes, you will.	No, you won't.
he'll help	he won't help	Will he help ...?	Yes, he will.	No, he won't.
she'll help	she won't help	Will she help ...?	Yes, she will.	No, she won't.
it'll help	it won't help	Will it help ...?	Yes, it will.	No, it won't.
we'll help	we won't help	Will we help ...?	Yes, we will.	No, we won't.
you'll help	you won't help	Will you help ...?	Yes, you will.	No, you won't.
they'll help	they won't help	Will they help ...?	Yes, they will.	No, they won't.

2 Complete the sentences with the correct form of the future simple. Use these verbs.

> be   depart   give   not come   pass   ~~stimulate~~

1 I'm sure the interactive whiteboard _____'ll/will stimulate_____ learning.

2 _____ the flight _____ on time?

3 The weather is awful! I _____ skiing with you.

4 Do you think our trip to India _____ a voyage of discovery?

5 _____ she _____ you some advice on where to stay?

6 You're an intelligent boy. I believe you _____ your exams.

Be going to

We use **be going to**
- to talk about future plans and intentions.
  Next summer, we're going to spend two months travelling around South America.
- to predict that something is going to happen when we have proof or information.
  Juliette is on the wrong platform. She's going to get on the wrong train!

Time expressions
We use the following **time expressions** with **be going to: tomorrow, in the morning/ afternoon/evening, this week/weekend, next week/month/year, in a week/month/ year,** etc.
Julie is going to buy a new car next week.

Affirmative	Negative	Question	Short answers	
I'm going to stay	I'm not going to stay	Am I going to stay ...?	Yes, I am.	No, I'm not.
you're going to stay	you aren't going to stay	Are you going to stay ...?	Yes, you are.	No, you're not.
he's going to stay	he isn't going to stay	Is he going to stay ...?	Yes, he is.	No, he isn't.
she's going to stay	she isn't going to stay	Is she going to stay ...?	Yes, she is.	No, she isn't.
it's going to stay	it isn't going to stay	Is it going to stay ...?	Yes, it is.	No, it isn't.
we're going to stay	we aren't going to stay	Are we going to stay ...?	Yes, we are.	No, we aren't.
you're going to stay	you aren't going to stay	Are you going to stay ...?	Yes, you are.	No, you aren't.
they're going to stay	they aren't going to stay	Are they going to stay ...?	Yes, they are.	No, they aren't.

3 Complete the dialogue with the correct form of *be going to*. Use the verbs in brackets.

Zoe: I'm so excited! This winter, my parents and I (1) _____are going to do_____ (do) something very exciting.

Oliver: (2) _____ (you / visit) your grandparents in the mountains?

Zoe: No, we (3) _____ (go) on an adventure holiday!
We (4) _____ (travel) to Norway for a husky safari.

Oliver: Oh. Where (5) _____ (you / stay)?

Zoe: In a cabin in the mountains. I can't wait. The travel agent says it's a relaxing holiday, but I
(6) _____ (not relax)! There
(7) _____ (be) so much to do!

Oliver: (8) _____ (you / ski) there?

Zoe: Of course. We can go cross-country skiing through forests and along rivers. We (9) _____ (visit) a reindeer farm, too!

Oliver: Wow, that sounds great!

Future continuous

We use the **future continuous**
- to talk about something that will be in progress at a specific time in the future.
  *In three weeks' time, we **'ll be learning** English at summer school.*
- to ask politely about someone's future plans.
  *Which cities **will** you **be visiting** during your trip around Europe?*
- to talk about plans that will definitely happen because they are routine or programmed actions.
  *It's Saturday today, so Sandy **will be having** lunch with her grandparents.*

Time expressions
We use the following **time expressions** with the **future continuous: in a few hours/days/weeks, in the near future, (this time) tomorrow, next week/month/year, soon, at seven o'clock tonight/tomorrow, during the weekend/summer, soon,** etc.
*George will be arriving **soon**.*

Affirmative	Negative	Question	Short answers	
I'll be working	I won't be working	Will I be working ...?	Yes, I will.	No, I won't.
you'll be working	you won't be working	Will you be working ...?	Yes, you will.	No, you won't.
he'll be working	he won't be working	Will he be working ...?	Yes, he will.	No, he won't.
she'll be working	she won't be working	Will she be working ...?	Yes, she will.	No, she won't.
it'll be working	it won't be working	Will it be working ...?	Yes, it will.	No, it won't.
we'll be working	we won't be working	Will we be working ...?	Yes, we will.	No, we won't.
you'll be working	you won't be working	Will you be working ...?	Yes, you will.	No, you won't.
they'll be working	they won't be working	Will they be working ...?	Yes, they will.	No, they won't.

4 Complete the sentences with the future continuous. Use the verbs in brackets.

1 This time next month, we __'ll/will be sitting__ on a sandy beach in the Caribbean. (sit)

2 In two hours' time, you _____ your flight to South Africa. (board)

3 This time tomorrow, my classmates and I _____ the Science Museum. (visit)

4 In the near future, my family and I _____ in a remote area any more. (not live)

5 In exactly ten minutes, we _____ the Swiss border. (cross)

6 Elisa is on holiday, so she _____ in the tournament this weekend. (not take part)

5 Write questions with the future continuous. Then complete the short answers.

1 ? / you / stay / at / a campsite

   __Will you be staying at a campsite?__

   Yes, _____I will_____ .

2 ? / the students / go / on their excursion / by coach

   _____

   _____

   No, _____ .

3 ? / Emily / help / you / with your research

   _____

   _____

   Yes, _____ .

4 ? / you / paint / your bedroom / this summer

   _____

   _____

   No, _____ .

5 ? / the agency / promote / creative holidays / this year

   _____

   _____

   Yes, _____ .

6 ? / I / present / the award / to / the travel writer

   _____

   _____

   No, _____ .

6 Circle the correct words.

1 I promise I **will be helping** / **will help** you with your homework this afternoon.

2 This time tomorrow, we **are going to explore** / **will be exploring** the sights in New York.

3 **Shall** / **Will** we sign up for the course to improve our English skills?

4 My sister and I have decided that we **are going to go** / **will be going** on a cruise around the Caribbean.

5 Have a look in the atlas and you **will find** / **will be finding** a map of Mozambique.

6 The police officers found some fingerprints, so they **are going to arrest** / **be arresting** the suspects.

7 Choose the correct answers.

1 Finish your homework or you _____ to Freddie's party tonight.
  a aren't going
  b won't go
  c be going to go

2 In two hours' time, we _____ in our car, on the way to summer camp!
  a will sit
  b are going to sit
  c will be sitting

3 _____ help me lift the suitcases into the car, please?
  a Will you be
  b Are you going
  c Will you

4 Mum, what _____ when Uncle Tom and Auntie Mary arrive?
  a we will be doing
  b are we doing
  c will we do

5 Jeremy _____ a flat in Vancouver next summer.
  a is going to rent
  b be renting
  c will renting

6 Oh no! I've got no petrol in the tank. The car _____ .
  a is going to stop
  b going to stop
  c will be stopping

8 Say it! Imagine that you are going on holiday. Talk with your partner about what you will be doing. Use the future simple, *be going to*, the future continuous and these suggestions to help you.

play beach volleyball

visit interesting places

eat lots of ice cream

relax in the sun

buy postcards

have fun swimming

I'll be relaxing in the sun.

I'm going to buy some postcards.

1 **Read.**

Soon, we'll have been walking for four hours and I can't see anything.

Don't worry. In a couple of hours, we'll have reached the campsite.

Future perfect simple

We use the **future perfect simple** to talk about something that will have finished
- before something else happens.
  We'll have reached the top of the mountain before it gets dark.
- before a specific time in the future.
  I'll have finished all my exams by the summer.

We form the **future perfect simple** with **will have** and the past participle of the verb. We use the same form for all persons of the verb.

See the list of past participles on page 159.

Time expressions
We use the following **time expressions** with the **future perfect simple: before, by seven o'clock/by now/ the weekend, by tomorrow/next week/summer, in a year's time, in ten minutes, soon,** etc.
*Samantha will have packed her suitcase **by tomorrow**.*

Affirmative	Negative	Question	Short answers	
I'll have arrived	I won't have arrived	Will I have arrived ...?	Yes, I will.	No, I won't.
you'll have arrived	you won't have arrived	Will you have arrived ...?	Yes, you will.	No, you won't.
he'll have arrived	he won't have arrived	Will he have arrived ...?	Yes, he will.	No, he won't.
she'll have arrived	she won't have arrived	Will she have arrived ...?	Yes, she will.	No, she won't.
it'll have arrived	it won't have arrived	Will it have arrived ...?	Yes, it will.	No, it won't.
we'll have arrived	we won't have arrived	Will we have arrived ...?	Yes, we will.	No, we won't.
you'll have arrived	you won't have arrived	Will you have arrived ...?	Yes, you will.	No, you won't.
they'll have arrived	they won't have arrived	Will they have arrived ...?	Yes, they will.	No, they won't.

2 **Look at the pictures and complete the sentences with the correct form of the future perfect simple. Use these verbs.**

choose   ~~iron~~   not eat   not paint   repair   wash

1 By six o'clock this evening, Mrs Jones _will have ironed_ all the clothes.

2 It's eleven o'clock. Henry _____ the house by midday.

3 _____ he _____ my car by the end of the day?

4 Johnny _____ his dinner by eight o'clock.

5 They _____ their mum's car by the end of the day.

6 _____ she _____ the destination by midnight tonight?

Future perfect continuous

We use the **future perfect continuous** to emphasise the duration of an activity that will be in progress before another time or event in the future.
By tomorrow morning, we'll have been trekking for three days.

We form the affirmative with **will have been** and the main verb with the ending **–ing** for all persons.
Karen will have been studying for five hours by the time she goes to bed.

In the negative form we use **won't have been** and the main verb with the ending **–ing**.
We won't have been doing our homework.

In the question form we use **will have been** and the main verb with the ending **–ing**. In short answers we only use **will**. We don't use the main verb.
Will you have been living in that house for ten years by 2020?
Yes, I will.

Note: The **future perfect continuous** is rarely used in the negative or question form.

Time expressions
We use the following **time expressions** with the **future perfect continuous: before, by seven o'clock/ by now/the weekend, by tomorrow/next week/summer, in a year's time, in ten minutes, soon,** etc.
By five o'clock, I'll have been answering emails for three hours.

Affirmative	Negative	Question	Short answers	
I'll have been trying	I won't have been trying	Will I have been trying ...?	Yes, I will.	No, I won't.
you'll have been trying	you won't have been trying	Will you have been trying ...?	Yes, you will.	No, you won't.
he'll have been trying	he won't have been trying	Will he have been trying ...?	Yes, he will.	No, he won't.
she'll have been trying	she won't have been trying	Will she have been trying ...?	Yes, she will.	No, she won't.
it'll have been trying	it won't have been trying	Will it have been trying ...?	Yes, it will.	No, it won't.
we'll have been trying	we won't have been trying	Will we have been trying ...?	Yes, we will.	No, we won't.
you'll have been trying	you won't have been trying	Will you have been trying ...?	Yes, you will.	No, you won't.
they'll have been trying	they won't have been trying	Will they have been trying ...?	Yes, they will.	No, they won't.

3 Complete the sentences with the future perfect continuous. Use the verbs in brackets.

1 Mum's been in the kitchen all morning. In ten minutes, she *'ll/will have been cooking* for three hours! (cook)

2 By August, we _____ in Dubai for four years. (live)

3 At three o'clock, the children _____ for two hours. (ski)

4 By the end of summer, the new band _____ Australia for three months. (tour)

5 Penny _____ Spanish for two years by the time she goes to university. (study)

6 By the end of the decade, the local community _____ this new sports complex for three years! (build)

4 Look at the list of duties for a school fête. Complete the sentences using the future perfect continuous.

Name		
Karen	sell tickets	10 a.m. – 1 p.m.
Lisa	sell cakes and drinks at the food stall	2 p.m. – 5 p.m.
Kerrie	help at the book stall	11 a.m. – 4 p.m.
Mr Peters	take children on pony rides	10 a.m. – 5 p.m.
Mrs Tate	supervise carnival rides	10 a.m. – 5 p.m.
Peter and Brian	organise competitions	11 a.m. – 4 p.m.

1 By one o'clock, Karen *will have been selling tickets for three hours* .

2 By three o'clock, Lisa _____ .

3 By midday, Kerrie _____ .

4 By the time the fête ends, Mr Peters _____ .

5 By five o'clock, Mrs Tate _____ .

6 By two o'clock, Peter and Brian _____ .

Future perfect simple or future perfect continuous?

We use the **future perfect simple** to emphasise that a future action will be completed and we use the **future perfect continuous** to emphasise the **duration** of a future action.
By four o'clock, we'll have packed our bags.
By four o'clock, we'll have been packing our bags for two hours.

5 Complete the sentences with the future perfect simple or the future perfect continuous. Use the verbs in brackets.

1 By midday tomorrow, we *'ll/will have arrived* at base camp. (arrive)

2 Soon, Hani _____ as captain of a cruise ship for six years. (work)

3 By August, my grandparents _____ Asia for two months. (explore)

4 In a month's time, I _____ all my final exams. (finish)

5 By summer, the annual expedition _____ . (begin)

6 We _____ for 12 hours by the time we land in Dubai. (fly)

6 Choose the correct answers.

1 We _____ the border to Mexico by seven o'clock this evening.

   a will have been crossing

   (b) will have crossed

   c will be crossing

2 By the time I finish the marathon, I _____ for seven hours.

   a will have been walking

   b will walk

   c will have walked

3 In 20 minutes, the divers _____ for three hours.

   a are

   b will have swum

   c will have been swimming

4 I _____ this volcano for days by the time I reach the crater.

   a will have been climbing

   b will have climbed

   c have climbed

5 By the New Year, Tim _____ as a guide in the Alps for six months.

   a will have been working

   b is working

   c will have worked

6 The archaeologists _____ their research by the end of their dig.

   a are completing

   b will have been completing

   c will have completed

7 Complete the telephone conversation with the future perfect simple or the future perfect continuous. Use the verbs in brackets.

> **Alex:** I'm exhausted today! By this time next week, I (1) _'ll/will have been backpacking_ (backpack) around India for six weeks!
>
> **Emily:** Wow! I (2) _____ (forget) what you look like by the time you get back!
>
> **Alex:** You certainly will! Elizabeth and I (3) _____ (lose) so much weight by then! We're not eating very much here.
>
> **Emily:** Which places have you visited so far?
>
> **Alex:** Well, we're still in Goa! In one week's time, I think we (4) _____ (explore) the whole region. It's just so beautiful.
>
> **Emily:** Is it carnival time there now?
>
> **Alex:** Yes, it is. The carnival lasts for another two days, so by the time it ends Elizabeth and I (5) _____ (celebrate) for three days!
>
> **Emily:** Apart from celebrating at the carnival, what else is there to do?
>
> **Alex:** Goa has spectacular beaches where you can relax. There are also old buildings and museums which are very interesting.
>
> **Emily:** I see. Are you planning to come home soon?
>
> **Alex:** Mm, yes. Soon, we (6) _____ (spend) all our money.
>
> **Emily:** OK! I can't wait to see you both.
>
> **Alex:** Bye!

8 Say it! Talk with a partner about what you will have done and what you will have been doing by the time you're 18. Use these suggestions to help you.

- finish school
- learn English / French
- live at home
- play sport / musical instrument
- start work
- go abroad

> I will have finished school by the time I'm 18.

> I will have been learning French for six years.

1 **Read.**

We're going to Australia!

Yes, we are. Our flight leaves at three o'clock.

I'll buy us some snacks for the flight.

Review of tenses: present simple and present continuous (future meaning)

We use the **present simple** to talk about timetabled and programmed events in the future.
*The cruise ship **sails** at seven o'clock in the morning.*

We use the **present continuous** to talk about fixed future plans.
We're going on safari in Kenya this summer.

2 **Complete the sentences with the correct form of the present simple or the present continuous. Use the verbs in brackets.**

1 Flight OA1923 to London _____departs_____ at seven o'clock in the morning. (depart)

2 What time _____ in the morning? (the bank / open)

3 I _____ to the football game tonight because I've got too much work. (not go)

4 _____ her grandparents this weekend? (Susan / visit)

5 The bus timetable has changed. The bus to Glasgow _____ at nine o'clock any more. (not leave)

6 There's a great film on TV later, so we _____ at home to watch it. (stay)

7 My train _____ at ten o'clock, so I need to leave now. (leave)

8 We _____ to London to see a musical this summer. (go)

Review of future tenses

Future simple

We use the **future simple**
- to make predictions.
  You'll have a wonderful time in Australia.
- to talk about decisions we make at the time of speaking.
  It's really cold tonight. I'll make some soup for dinner.
- to make offers, promises, threats or to give warnings.
  Be careful! You'll hurt yourself.
  I'll make you a cup of tea.
  I'll come straight home after school.
  I'll report you to the head teacher if you're late again.
- to ask someone to do something for us.
  Will you answer the phone, please?
- to state opinions for the future after **think, hope, be sure, believe, bet** and **probably**.
  Dad believes he'll get the job.

Be going to

We use **be going to**
- to talk about future plans and intentions.
  We're going to ride in a hot air balloon on Sunday.
- to predict that something is going to happen when we have proof or information.
  The pavement is very slippery. I'm going to fall over!

Future continuous

We use the **future continuous**
- to talk about something that will be in progress at a specific time in the future.
  In a month's time, Suzie will be working in her dad's office.
- to ask politely about someone's future plans.
  What time will you be interviewing the candidates?

3 Look at these situations and write what these people would say. Use the correct form of the future simple, *be going to* or the future continuous.

1 It's Friday and John and Cathy are in class. They are talking about going to the beach the next day at the same time.
  <u>This time tomorrow, we'll be going to the beach.</u>

2 Your sister is hungry. You offer to make her a sandwich.
  _____

3 Mum is washing the dishes when somebody knocks on the door. She asks her daughter to open the door.
  _____

4 Mr Tate is looking up at the sky. There are many dark clouds.
  _____

5 You don't know what your teacher is planning to give you for homework, but you want to find out.
  _____

6 Your best friend sees a beautiful T-shirt, but she decides not to buy it.
  _____

7 You and your dad are talking about your flight to London at the same time next week.
  _____

8 You have seen *Iceberg 3* and you really enjoyed it. You are sure that your friend will too.
  _____

9 Paul isn't working at the moment but in one month's time he will be. He was offered a job in a travel agency.
  _____

10 There is a party tomorrow. You and your family have been invited and you plan to go.
  _____

4 Complete the dialogue with the correct form of the verbs in brackets. Use the present simple, the present continuous, the future simple, *be going to* or the future continuous.

Eva: Guess what we (1) __'re doing / 're going to do__ (do) this afternoon

Billy: I don't know!

Eva: We (2) _____ (tour) around London on a double-decker bus.

Billy: Wow! What time (3) _____ (the bus / leave)?

Eva: At four o'clock. In two hours' time, we (4) _____ (admire) the sights of London from the top of a bus!

Billy: Which sights (5) _____ (you / visit)?

Eva: Oh, Westminster, Buckingham Palace, Big Ben of course and maybe Tower Bridge. But I'm worried it might rain.

Billy: Don't worry! There isn't a cloud in the sky. It (6) _____ (rain)! I'm sure you (7) _____ (have) a wonderful time.

Eva: I hope so! Billy, could you do something for me?

Billy: What is it?

Eva: (8) _____ (you / help) me with my homework tomorrow?

Review of future tenses

Future perfect simple

We use the **future perfect simple** to talk about an action that will have been completed before another action or before a specific time in the future.
*By the time you wake up, **I'll have cleaned** the whole house!*

Future perfect continous

We use the **future perfect continuous** to talk about how long an action will have been in progress by a specific time in the future.
*By midday, the local citizens **will have been protesting** for three hours.*

5 Circle the correct words.

1 By the end of summer, we **'ll have moved** / will have been moving to our new house.

2 There is a lot of traffic. They **won't have arrived** / **won't have been arriving** by four o'clock.

3 Will the helicopter tour **have finished** / **have been finishing** by six o'clock this evening?

4 By June, the schoolchildren **will have collected** / **will have been collecting** money for the charity for nine months.

5 Don't worry. Jane **won't have waited** / **won't have been waiting** for long by the time you arrive.

6 Will Victoria **have completed** / **have been completing** her project by five o'clock?

6 **The words in bold are wrong. Write the correct words.**

1 The athlete is sure he will **be breaking** the world record this year.   _____break_____

2 This time tomorrow, we will **have been** sailing around the Canary Islands.   _____

3 In ten years' time, the scientist will **work** on this project for 15 years.   _____

4 The film **start** at nine o'clock.   _____

5 Will you have **finish** your homework by the time I get home tonight?   _____

6 By this time tomorrow, we will **arrive** at our destination.   _____

7 **Choose the correct answers.**

1 This time tomorrow, Dan and Sandy _____ in the 100-metre race.

   a are competing
   b will be competing
   c will have compete

2 The athletes _____ for three hours by the time the marathon finishes.

   a run
   b will have run
   c will have been running

3 Hurry! The performance _____ at seven o'clock.

   a will have started
   b will have been starting
   c starts

4 I bet you _____ a wonderful time at the party.

   a are going to have
   b will have
   c will have had

5 Dad promises he _____ me a moped for my seventeenth birthday.

   a will buy
   b will have bought
   c buys

6 We have decided that we _____ in a camper van this summer.

   a aren't going to travel
   b don't travel
   c won't have been travelling

7 _____ in the swimming race next weekend?

   a Do you take part
   b Will you have taken part
   c Are you taking part

8 _____ extinct by 2025?

   a Will this species have become
   b Is this species
   c Is this species being

8 **Say it! Talk with your partner about your plans for the future. Use these suggestions to help you.**

- go to university
- learn to drive
- start work
- buy a car
- take up a new sport
- travel abroad

I'll be going to university in ten years' time.

I'm going to learn to drive.

1 Read.

> Dad, can I buy some chocolate?

> No, you can't. The last time you ate chocolate you weren't able to finish your dinner!

Can

We use **can**
- to talk about ability in the present.
  *Marcus **can run** very fast.*
- to ask or give permission.
  ***Can** I **dive** into the pool now?*
  *Yes, you **can** play my new game.*
- to talk about possibility.
  *We **can** jog around the park every morning.*
- for requests and suggestions.
  ***Can** you come with me to the doctor's, please?*

We usually use **can't** instead of **cannot** in everyday English, but we sometimes use **cannot** to give emphasis.
*No, Susan, you **cannot** take all your brother's sweets!*

Can is followed by the bare infinitive.
*My mum **can speak** three foreign languages.*

We often use **can** and **could** with verbs of the senses such as **see**, **hear**, **smell**, etc.
*I **can see** the keys, they're on the kitchen table.*
*I **could** smell the spaghetti bolognaise from my bedroom!*

Could

We use **could**
- to talk about ability in the past.
  *Rosie **could swim** when she was four years old!*
- to ask permission in the present or the future.
  ***Could** I go to the park after school?*
- to ask for something politely.
  ***Could** I have a glass of water, please?*
- for requests and suggestions.
  *You **could** take up yoga to help you relax.*

We don't use **could** for abilities in the past when we talk about a specific occasion when we managed to do something. In this case, we use **was able to** or **were able to**.
*I didn't have much time, but **I was able** to finish my work.*

However, we can use **couldn't** to talk about specific situations in the past.
*I **couldn't** get through to Jane last night.*

Could is followed by the bare infinitive.
*Mrs Taylor **could swim** very fast when she was younger.*

Remember!

Can and could are the same for all persons.
I **can** sing. I **could** dive.
You **can** sing. You **could** dive.

Be able to

We use **be able to**
- to talk about ability.
  *Sandra **is able to** speak three languages.*
- to talk about a specific occasion when we managed or didn't manage to do something.
  *I **was able to** finish all my chores today.*
  (We can't use **could** here.)
  *I **wasn't able to** start the report this morning.*
  (We can also use **couldn't** here.)

We can use **be able to** with many tenses; we just use the correct form of the verb **be**. But we don't use **be able to** with continuous tenses.

Be able to is followed by the bare infinitive.
*All the children **were able to** complete their projects on time.*

2 Circle the correct words.

1 My grandma (could) / **was able** sing very well when she was younger.

2 Mrs Stevens, **can I / am I able to** ask you a question?

3 Sorry, I **could / wasn't able to** finish my project.

4 We **can / are able to** go to the park if you like.

5 Lyn is an interpreter. She **can / could** speak three languages.

6 I **can / am able** to hear you, but I can't see you.

Would

We use **would** in the question form
- for requests.
  ***Would** you help me with the cooking?*
- when asking for permission.
  ***Would** you mind if I bring a friend to the party?*

We use **would** to ask more politely. When we answer a question with **would**, we use **will**.
***Would** you drive me home, please?*
*Yes, I **will**.*

Would is followed by a noun or subject pronoun and the bare infinitive.
***Would George mind** if I used his phone?*
***Would you write** down your name and address?*

3 Complete the sentences with the correct form of *can, could, be able to* or *would* and these verbs.

come   do   not clean   ~~not go~~   not stay   turn off

1 Yesterday, Mum wasn't well, so she _wasn't able to/couldn't go_ to the office.

2 _____ you _____ the computer, please?

3 I'm tired, so I _____ the windows for you.

4 We _____ some stretching exercises while we are waiting for our coach to arrive.

5 _____ you and Katie _____ for a bike ride with me?

6 Julie tries so hard, but she _____ in shape.

Must and can't (for certainty)

We use **must** to say that we are sure that something is true.
*Uncle Harry **must** be fit. He's been jogging for hours!*

We use **can't** to say that we are sure that something is not true.
*You **can't** be exhausted. You've been sleeping all morning!*

Must and **can't** are followed by the bare infinitive.
*You **must be** tired. You've been working all day.*
*Alexander **can't be** hungry. He ate four slices of pizza.*

4 **Match.**

1 Aisha's mum is an aerobics teacher.
2 George can't swim yet.
3 Jamie and Jemma have been studying all morning.
4 Our science teacher is away on holiday.
5 Samantha has always wanted to be on stage.
6 The band's song was awful.

a They can't be the winners of the song contest!
b They must be exhausted now.
c She must be very fit!
d That can't be her over there!
e That can't be him in the pool.
f That must be her in the school play.

Must

We can also use **must** to talk about obligation and necessity in the present and in the future.
*We **must** always stop at a red light.*
*I **must** post the letter tomorrow.*

We use **mustn't** to talk about something that we are not allowed to do in the present and in the future.
*We **mustn't** park here.*
*They **mustn't** arrive late for the meeting tomorrow.*

Must and **mustn't** are followed by the bare infinitive.
*I **must finish** my work tonight.*
*I **mustn't use** a pen in the exam.*

We can't use **must** for the past. We use **had to**.
*I **had to** complete my assignment last night.*

Must isn't usually used in questions. To ask if someone is obliged to do something, we use the question form of **have to**.
***Does** she **have to** reply to all these emails?*

Have to

We use **have to** in a variety of tenses to talk about an obligation in the present, future and in the past.
*We **have to** look after ourselves.*

Have to is followed by the bare infinitive.
*Mum **has to cook** a lot of food for the party.*

Need to and needn't

We use **need to** in a variety of tenses to talk about necessity in the present, future and in the past.
*I **will need to** complete this report.*

We use **needn't** to talk about a lack of necessity in the present.
*You **needn't buy** some milk. Dan has already bought some.*

Need to and **needn't** are followed by the bare infinitive.
*Fred **needs to hand in** his assignment.*
*You **needn't cook** anything as Jenny is taking us out for dinner.*

Mustn't vs don't have to

Mustn't and **don't have to** have a totally different meaning. We use **mustn't** to say that we are not allowed to do something.
*We **mustn't talk** in the library.*

We use **don't have to** to say that it isn't necessary to do something, but we can do it if we want to.
*You **don't have to** go swimming if you don't want to.*

Mustn't and **don't have to** are followed by the bare infinitive.
*You **mustn't wake** the baby.*
*You **don't have to cook** dinner.*

5 Complete the sentences with the correct form of *must, mustn't, have to, don't have to* or *needn't* and the verbs in brackets. Sometimes more than one answer is possible.

1 You _don't have to/needn't cook_ tonight. I've ordered Chinese. (cook)

2 I _____ eating a burger a day! I've got very high cholesterol. (stop)

3 We _____ our dancing lesson. Our teacher gets very angry! (miss)

4 I'm so glad I _____ lunch at school yesterday! The food was awful! (eat)

5 Last year, Dad _____ on a diet. None of his clothes fitted him! (go)

6 I _____ to buy some lettuce for the salad. (forget)

6 Circle the correct words.

> Nowadays, we are all very busy and we have very little free time. This is why we (1) **must /(have)** to eat healthily and exercise whenever we (2) **can / could**.
>
> We (3) **mustn't / needn't** eat too many convenience foods, and we (4) **have to / will be able to** make sure we eat a lot of fruit and vegetables.
>
> In the past, we (5) **could / can** just walk to school or work, but now we drive everywhere so we 6) **must / were able to** take up a sport. This (7) **needn't be / couldn't be** a strenuous sport if you don't have very much energy.
>
> We (8) **mustn't / don't have** get used to a sedentary lifestyle as we'll put on weight.
>
> The next time you look in the mirror and say 'Oh! This (9) **can't be / must be** me. I am so overweight!', think about the advice I have just given you. You (10) **could / will be able** to see the difference in no time!

7 Look at the situations and complete the sentences using an appropriate phrase which includes a modal verb.

1 The travel agent said we would stay at a luxury hotel. We have just arrived and we are shocked as there isn't even a wardrobe in the room!

This _____ can't be _____ a luxury hotel.

2 We are on holiday and there's lots of food in the camper van for us to eat.

We _____ at a restaurant tonight.

3 Last night I made a pizza because I had tomatoes, olives and peppers.

I _____ a pizza last night.

4 Two young people see a young man playing tennis. He is playing very well.

He _____ a professional tennis player.

5 A lady is looking at her daughter swinging on monkey bars. She remembers doing the same thing when she was a little girl.

I _____ on monkey bars when I was my daughter's age.

6 A family is at an amusement park. The little girl wants to go on the rollercoaster, but she isn't tall enough.

She _____ the rollercoaster because she isn't tall enough.

8 Rewrite the sentences using the words given. Use between two and five words.

1 It is necessary that you cut down on chocolate. **to**

You _____ have to _____ cut down on chocolate.

2 Anna has broken her leg, so I'm sure she's not at the aerobics class. **can't**

Anna has broken her leg, so _____ at the aerobics class.

3 When I was younger, I could do the splits. **was**

When I was younger, I _____ do the splits.

4 Don't do the vacuuming; I've already done it. **needn't**

You _____ the vacuuming.

5 I'm sure there's an escalator at the shopping mall. **must**

There _____ at the shopping mall.

6 Dad had a check-up six months ago, so he doesn't need to have another one. **have**

Dad _____ to have another check-up.

9 Say it! Imagine you are at summer camp. Talk to your partner about these things using modals.

- wake up at eight o'clock
- play various sports
- eat everything on our lunch tray
- take part in arts and crafts
- make our beds
- tidy our room
- sweep the floor
- play board games in the evening
- go to sleep at ten o'clock

We have to wake up at eight o'clock.

We can play various sports.

1 Read.

> May I leave the table?

> No, you should finish your food first.

May and might

We use **may** and **might** to show possibility.
*We **may** eat out tonight.*
*I **might** go to the concert this weekend.*

We use **may** to ask for and to give permission.
***May** I buy a packet of crisps, Mum?*
*Yes, you **may** have some ice cream.*

May and **might** are followed by the bare infinitive.
*Keith **may come** over tonight.*
*We **might watch** a film after dinner.*

> **Remember !**
>
> We don't use the question form of **might** and we usually say **might not** instead of **mightn't**. I don't feel well. I **might not** go to the party.

2 Look at the pictures and complete the sentences with the correct form of *may* or *might* and these verbs.

| ~~be~~ book buy go |

1 Thomas _may/might be_ allergic to nuts.

2 No, you _____ a new toy car.

3 _____ we _____ on a first-aid course?

4 My classmates and I _____ a table at the new restaurant.

Should

We use should
- to give advice.
  You **should** eat more healthily.
  You **shouldn't** play computer games all day.
- to ask for advice.
  Should I complain to the manager?
- to make a prediction.
  It's an easy recipe. I **should** be able to make the casserole.

Should is followed by the bare infinitive.
You **should exercise** more often.

Ought to

We use **ought to** to give advice.
We all **ought to do** more exercise.
Dan **ought not to** eat cheese if he's allergic to it.

Ought to isn't used in the question form.

Ought to is followed by the bare infinitive.
Brian **ought to tidy** his room more often.

3 Read the problems and give advice. Use *should, shouldn't, ought to* or *ought not to* and these verbs. Sometimes more than one answer is possible.

> donate   ~~eat~~   sit   read   take   walk

1 I usually have eggs and pancakes for breakfast. I know it's not healthy, but breakfast is my favourite meal.

You ____should/ought to eat____ cereal for breakfast.

2 My friends and I are very busy and we don't have time to take up a sport. Our parents drive us to school every morning.

You and your friends _____ to school.

3 When I get home from school, I'm exhausted. I just want to watch a little TV, but when I finish doing my homework, it's time for bed.

You _____ in front of the TV all afternoon.

4 Mum's in the office all day. She doesn't have time to exercise.

She _____ the stairs.

5 I always eat health food bars, but it seems that they are high in calories, too.

You _____ the nutritional information on the packet.

6 I've got lots of old clothes and shoes. I don't know what to do with them.

You _____ your old clothes to charity.

4 Circle the correct words.
1 (May) / Should I come to the art gallery with you, please?
2 We **ought not / shouldn't** to drop litter in the park.
3 **Ought to / Should** supermarkets and department stores be open every day?
4 **Might / May** I have a bunch of bananas and half a watermelon, please?
5 You really **should / may** recycle batteries, too.
6 Isabel **should / ought** keep the pet tarantula in the garden.

5 Complete the telephone conversation. Use *should, ought, may* or *might*.

Alison: Dr Hansen, I've been feeling awful for a couple of days and I think I (1) _____may/might_____ have the flu. What (2) _____ I do?

Dr Hansen: Well, the first thing you (3) _____ to check is whether you've got a temperature or not.

Alison: I see. (4) _____ I book an appointment to see you, please?

Dr Hansen: Well, you (5) _____ not get out of bed really, as you (6) _____ get worse.

Alison: OK, well, (7) _____ I take some antibiotics?

Dr Hansen: You don't need antibiotics if it's just a common cold. What you really (8) _____ to do is relax, eat healthily and make sure you drink orange juice. You (9) _____ not feel better immediately, but in a couple of days, you (10) _____ be well enough to go back to work. If you still feel ill in a couple of days, call me and I'll come and see you.

Alison: OK, thank you.

6 Rewrite the sentences using the words given. Use between two and five words.

1 It's possible that Gina has got asthma. **may**

   Gina _____may have_____ asthma.

2 It's not a good idea to eat products that contain lots of sugar. **to**

   You _____ eat products that contain lots of sugar.

3 Is it all right if I order dessert? **can**

   _____ order dessert?

4 It isn't a good idea to drink fizzy drinks. **not**

   You _____ drink fizzy drinks.

5 We believe that Ian will pass his final exams. **should**

   Ian _____ final exams.

6 I probably won't go to the party tonight. **not**

   I _____ come to the party tonight.

7 Say it! Talk with your partner about what advice you would give in these situations using the correct form of *may, might, should* or *ought to*.

Situation 1

Paul doesn't like meat but he needs to eat proteins. What should or shouldn't he do?

Situation 2

Brad has put on lots of weight. He has tried dieting but it hasn't worked so far. What ought he to do and what other options might he try?

Situation 3

Maggie wants to take up a sport but she doesn't like strenuous sports. Which sports might she like?

Situation 4

Giselle and Hannah love sweets. They're young but they already have tooth decay. What should they do to stop eating sweets?

Paul should eat fish and nuts.

Brad ought to do more exercise.

1 **Read.**

> Wow, this food looks amazing. You shouldn't have gone to so much trouble.

> Yes, this must have taken you ages!

Modal perfect forms

We can use modal verbs with **have** and a past participle to talk about past actions and states.

Possibility

We use **could have + past participle** to talk about something that was possible in the past but didn't happen.
*Why did you eat the whole cake? You **could have made** yourself sick.*

We use **may/might have + past participle** to talk about something that was possible in the past, but we don't know whether it happened or not.
*Isabel **might have wanted** to take up a new hobby.*
*My little brother **may have broken** the glass.*

Deduction

We use **must have been + past participle** when we feel sure something was true in the past.
*Natalie got 100% for her French exam. She **must have studied** very hard.*

We use **can't/couldn't + past participle** when we feel sure that something was not true in the past.
*You **can't have seen** Tom at the sports centre. He's in Germany!*
*Harry **couldn't have made** this meal. He can't even boil an egg!*

Criticism

We use **shouldn't have/ought not to have + past participle** to talk about something that we disapproved of in the past.
*Timothy **shouldn't have drunk** the whole bottle of lemonade.*
*You **ought not to have been** so rude to the salesman.*

2 **Circle the correct words.**

1 You **can't have seen** / **must have seen** Sally yesterday. She's been in hospital since Friday.

2 Steve **could have helped** / **can't have helped** with the preparations, but he didn't.

3 The living room looks great! The children **ought not to have tidied** / **must have tidied** it!

4 You really **shouldn't have taken** / **may have taken** Katie's ball.

5 George **must have got** / **can't have got** a new job. He's bought a really expensive car.

6 The children **might have** / **ought to have** wanted another drink.

3 Look at these situations and complete the sentences using the words given. Use between two and five words.

1 Tommy finished a whole pizza, and now he can't move! **shouldn't**

Tommy _____shouldn't have eaten_____ so much pizza.

2 We had a lot of homework, but James said that he finished it all in 15 minutes. I don't believe him! **have**

James _____ the homework in 15 minutes.

3 Paul accidentally dropped his father's laptop. He thinks it might be broken. **broken**

Dad, _____ your laptop. I'm not sure though.

4 My colleagues throw away lots of paper. It's such a waste. **to**

My colleagues _____ away the paper.

5 It's possible that they bought a house in the countryside. **may**

They _____ in the countryside.

6 I left my sandwich on the table and when I returned, it had disappeared. My little brother was sleeping nearby. **must**

My little brother _____ the sandwich.

7 I hadn't studied, so I looked at Carrie's answers during the test. Now we're both in trouble. **have**

You _____ Carrie's answers during the test.

8 We took the boat to the island and it took ages! It would have been a better idea to fly there. **could**

You _____ to the island instead.

4 Look at the pictures and complete the sentences with the correct perfect modal form. Use these verbs. Sometimes more than one answer is possible.

> fall   make   not put   ~~not stay~~   send   solve

1 Kids, you _shouldn't have stayed_ up so late!

2 My mum _____ the cake while I was at school!

3 The little boy _____ _____ the puzzle.

4 You _____ all your toys on the floor!

5 Faye and Mel _____ these flowers for my birthday.

6 Why did you put the baby on the chair? He _____ .

77

5 Choose the correct answers.

1 This chicken is tasteless! I _____ to add salt.

   (a) may have forgotten

   b should have forgotten

   c ought to have forgotten

2 Sandra _____ started dieting. She looks much slimmer now.

   a can't have

   b ought to have

   c must have

3 There's too much butter in this cake. You _____ to have used my recipe.

   a ought

   b could

   c may

4 We really _____ all those biscuits.

   a couldn't have eaten

   b mustn't have eaten

   c shouldn't have eaten

5 Rosemary can't sing very well. She _____ the talent contest.

   a must have won

   b can't have won

   c should have won

6 Peter _____ a car. I don't see him at the bus stop any more.

   a can't have bought

   b must have bought

   c ought to have bought

6 Complete the dialogue with these words.

can't have digested   could have ended up   may have forgotten
must have eaten   ought to have listened   ~~shouldn't have played~~

Dora: Are you OK, Max?

Max: I am now, but I (1) ___shouldn't have played___ in the volleyball match.

Dora: Why? What happened?

Max: I had lunch at one o'clock and the match was at two. Mum told me not to play, and I (2) _____ to her. During the match, I felt awful. The coach (3) _____ that I had told him I had just eaten and he told me to play.

Dora: Oh dear.

Max: Yes, I (4) _____ lunch too quickly.

Dora: In an hour, you (5) _____ your food, can you?

Max: Exactly. I (6) _____ in hospital. Now I know next time. No food before a match.

7 Say it! Imagine that something has disappeared from your bedroom. Talk with your partner about what disappeared and what may have happened to it. Use these suggestions and the perfect modal form.

- threw it away accidentally
- Mum put it in a drawer
- left it at a friend's house
- sister hid it

I can't have thrown my iPod away accidentally.

Mum may have put my iPod in a drawer.

1 Complete the sentences with the correct form of the future simple, *be going to* or the future continuous. Use the verbs in brackets.

1 Lizzie promises she _____won't take up_____ an extreme sport. (not take up)

2 In a few years, we _____ new sources of energy. (use)

3 Look! Tina is first, she _____ the swimming race. (win)

4 Turn down the volume on your computer or I _____ it _____ . (turn off)

5 What _____ in three hours' time? (you / do)

6 Sam has decided that she _____ as a volunteer this summer. (not work)

7 I can't wait! This time next week, I _____ in the sea. (swim)

8 Mum, _____ me to school tomorrow? (you / drive)

2 Make sentences. Use the future perfect simple or the future perfect continuous.

1 soon / I / pick up / every plastic bottle / on this beach

_____Soon I will have picked up every plastic bottle on this beach._____

2 ? / the temperature / reach / minus ten / by tonight

_____

3 Grandma's flight / not land / in ten minutes

_____

4 I / not get / my driving licence / by the end of the year

_____

5 on 1st March / we / live / in our flat / for six years

_____

6 by six o'clock / I / tidy / my room / for two hours

_____

3 Complete the sentences using future tenses. Use the verbs in brackets. Sometimes more than one answer is possible.

1 I bet Dad _____will forget_____ to buy me an MP4 player for my birthday. (forget)

2 In two years' time, the biologist _____ his research. (complete)

3 This time next week, we _____ from university! (graduate)

4 Can we go now? In ten minutes, we _____ in this cave for two hours! (hide)

5 Jo has decided she _____ in the competition next week. (not take part)

6 It's too cold to walk to school. I think I _____ the bus. (catch)

4 **Circle the correct words.**

1 **(Would you)/ Are you able to** lend me your rucksack, please?

2 Unfortunately, we **couldn't / won't be able to** visit our grandparents at the farm next weekend.

3 I tried very hard, but I **can't / wasn't able to** finish the crossword.

4 My little sister **can't / couldn't** ride a horse until she was 11 years old.

5 We **can / couldn't** take the catamaran or the ferry.

6 **Could you / You are able to** drive me to the leisure centre, please?

5 **Complete the sentences with *can't be* or *must be*.**

1 She doesn't speak German. She _____ can't be _____ a German teacher!

2 Roger has been working on his experiment all day. He _____ tired.

3 Natasha always does well in tests. She _____ a good student.

4 That _____ your mobile phone. It's mine!

5 Eric has gone on holiday for a week. He _____ happy!

6 Dina hasn't eaten much all day. She _____ on a diet.

6 **Choose the correct answers.**

1 I've got a map, so we _____ ask for directions.
   (a) needn't
   b mustn't
   c don't have

2 _____ book a cabin on the cruise ship?
   a Do we have to
   b We ought to
   c We have to

3 If you don't like fairgrounds, you _____ to come with me.
   a mustn't
   b needn't
   c don't have

4 You were very lucky. You _____ hurt yourself.
   a shouldn't
   b could have
   c could

5 I failed the maths test, so I _____ retake it yesterday.
   a must
   b had to
   c must have

6 This water is very dirty, so you _____ drink it.
   a mustn't
   b don't have
   c ought

7 John got a bike for his birthday, so he _____ walk to school any more.
   a doesn't have to
   b needs
   c mustn't

8 Jennifer _____ to say she wasn't coming.
   a don't have to call
   b should call
   c ought to have called

7 **Complete the text. Use these words. Sometimes more than one answer is possible.**

> may   may not   might not   ~~must~~   ought   should

To all students taking part in the field trip

You (1) _____ **must** _____ all be outside the school gates at 7.30 a.m. on Saturday, 11th June.

If you want, you (2) _____ bring a friend with you, but make sure you tell the head

teacher, Mrs Mullane, by Wednesday, as there (3) _____ be any seats left on the

coach. Don't forget to have some breakfast before you leave, as we (4) _____

have time to stop on the way. You (5) _____ wear comfortable clothes; girls

(6) _____ not to wear heels, as we'll be climbing up hills and crossing streams.

WRITING PROJECT

8 **Look at a project about health and fitness. Complete the project with these words.**

> can see   have to eat   might be   must be   ~~must have known~~   need to stop   ought
> should cut down   should eat   will continue   will have reached   will have finished

A healthy mind in a healthy body

In the ancient world, people (1) ___ **must have known** ___ what they were talking about when they said 'a healthy mind means a healthy body'.

Nowadays, we all know that the key factors to well-being are a balanced diet and exercise. This doesn't mean that we (2) _____ eating our favourite foods. We just (3) _____ in moderation. We (4) _____ a lot of fruit and vegetables, but we (5) _____ on carbohydrates and sugars. As well as a healthy diet, we (6) _____ to make sure that we exercise whenever we have the chance. Walking, jogging, playing a team sport on a regular basis and even everyday household chores are just some of the activities that help us maintain a healthy body.

Many people have started to include physical activities in their leisure time. Take this father and son, for instance. We (7) _____ that they are hiking on a mountain. They (8) _____ on a day hike, which means that they (9) _____ the hike by the end of the day and won't stay anywhere overnight. In a moment, they (10) _____ the top of the mountain and the two of them (11) _____ their hike. They (12) _____ enjoying themselves as they are spending quality time together.

9 **Now it's your turn to do a project about health and fitness. Find or draw a picture of an aspect of health and fitness and write about it.**

1 Read.

If it's a sunny day, we'll go to the beach.

Conditional sentences

Conditional sentences have got two clauses: an *if* clause and a *result* clause. It doesn't matter which clause comes first, but if the *if* clause comes first, we use a comma.
If it's a nice day, *we'll go to the beach.*
We'll go to the beach **if it's a nice day***.*

When we form negative conditional sentences, the negative form can be used in one or both clauses.
If you **don't know** *Cathy's address, I'll tell you.*
If James **doesn't have** *breakfast, he* **won't have** *any energy.*

But when we form conditional questions, the question form is only used in the result clause.
Will *you* **go** *to the park if you have time?*

Zero conditional

We use the **zero conditional** to talk about facts and general truths.
If you exercise, you feel good.

We use the **present simple** in both the *if* clause and the *result* clause.
If you **heat** *water to 100°C, it* **boils***.*

Note: We can use **when** instead of **if** with the zero conditional.
When I **don't sleep** *enough, I* **get** *a headache.*

2 Complete the sentences with the zero conditional. Use the verbs in brackets.

1 If you ___recycle___ , you ___help___ the planet. (recycle, help)

2 I _____ well in exams when I _____ . (do, revise)

3 If you _____ Russia during winter, the weather _____ very cold. (visit, be)

4 Plants _____ if you _____ them regularly. (grow, water)

5 If we _____ the air-conditioning on all day, it _____ a lot of electricity. (leave, consume)

6 When you _____ the spell check on your computer, you _____ making spelling mistakes. (use, avoid)

First conditional

We use the **first conditional** to talk about things that are likely to happen in the present or in the future.
*If you **miss** the bus, **you'll be** late for work.*

The *if* clause uses **if** and the **present simple**, the **present continuous** or the **present perfect continuous,** and the *result* clause uses the **future simple**.
*If I **take** the bus to work, I **will save** money on petrol.*
*If you **are looking** for Josh, you**'ll find** him in the library.*
*If they **haven't heard** the news yet, I**'ll tell** them.*

We can use modal verbs like **can, must** and **may** instead of **will**.
*If I miss the seven o'clock bus, I **may be** late.*

We can use **unless** with the first conditional to mean **if not**.
***If** we don't make an effort, we won't find alternative sources of energy.*
***Unless** we make an effort, we won't find alternative sources of energy.*

We can also use **provided/providing (that)** and **as long as** with the first conditional.
***Providing (that)** you don't have any homework, you can go out.*
*You can go swimming **as long as** the sea is clean.*

We can use imperatives in either clause of a first conditional sentence.
*If you've finished, **go** home.*
***Finish** quickly, and I will let you go home.*

3 Write sentences with the first conditional.

1 you / have / more job opportunities / if / you / speak / foreign / languages
   <u>You will have more job opportunities if you speak foreign languages.</u>

2 unless / it / rain / there / be / a drought
   _____

3 as long as / Amani / try hard / she / succeed
   _____

4 if / I / improve / my general knowledge / I / feel / much happier
   _____

5 Jason / get / the position / providing / he / know / Spanish
   _____

6 we / not / go / on a picnic / unless / it / be / a nice day
   _____

7 if / I / pass / my exams / I / go / to / university / next year
   _____

8 Dad / bake / a cake / if / he / have / time / this evening
   _____

Second conditional

We use the **second conditional**
- to talk about something that is unlikely to happen in the present or in the future.
  *We**'d travel** the world if we **had** enough money.*
- to talk about something which is impossible in the present or in the future.
  *If the sun's rays **weren't** so harmful, I**'d swim** all day long!*
- to give advice.
  *If I **were** you, I**'d exercise** more.*

The *if* clause uses **if** and the **past simple** and the *result* clause uses **would/could** and the **bare infinitive**.
*If we **lived** in the city centre, we **wouldn't need** a car.*

Remember !

We usually use **were** instead of **was** in second conditional sentences.
If I **were** more adventurous, I'd try parachuting.

4 **Complete the sentences with the second conditional. Use the verbs in brackets.**

1 If we ____didn't use____ our cars so much, we ___'d/would reduce___ pollution. (not use, reduce)

2 I _____ recyclable products if I _____ more time. (collect, have)

3 If we _____ the lights for one hour a day, _____ a difference? (turn off, it / make)

4 Daniel _____ to the sports centre if he _____ in such a remote area.
(walk, not live)

5 _____ me with my research if I _____ you? (you / help, pay)

6 We _____ if our neighbours _____ so noisy! (not complain, not be)

5 **Choose the correct answers.**

1 If the power station emitted less pollution, our
town _____ so polluted.

   a isn't
   (b) wouldn't be
   c won't be

2 Providing we all _____ an effort, we can stop
climate change.

   a would make
   b will make
   c make

3 _____ temperature decrease if we stop burning
fossil fuels?

   a Will the Earth's
   b Has the Earth's
   c Is the Earth's

4 When we _____ some exercise, we feel really good
and we sleep better.

   a will do
   b do
   c would do

5 If you _____ a shower instead of a bath, you
save water.

   a have
   b would have
   c has

6 If _____ proper cycling lanes, more people would
cycle.

   a there were
   b there would be
   c there was

6 **Complete the text with the zero, first or second conditional. Use the verbs in brackets.**

If we (1) _____want_____ (want) to achieve something,
we do our best to make it happen. If we had to stop
climate change today, we (2) _____ (spend) all
our time looking into renewable sources of energy and how
they can be used. Let's take wind power, for example. It's not
new; people have been using it for many years. Windmills
were used and are still used to grind grain or pump water.
Nowadays, wind turbines are also used in many places
around the world. When the wind turns the blades which are
connected to a shaft, it (3) _____ (spin) an electric
generator to produce electricity.
One or two wind turbines can't make a difference, though. Unless
more companies build wind farms which contain many wind turbines,
we (4) _____ (not see) a huge change. Wind farms are a
simple solution; providing areas (5) _____ (have) plenty of
wind, they can be built almost anywhere. If we build many of these wind
farms, we (6) _____ (succeed) in producing enough energy for
millions of people around the world.

7 **Look at the situations and write conditional sentences. Use the words in bold.**

1 You have a lot of homework. You can't go to your friend's house before you finish it. **if**
   If I don't finish my homework, I can't go to my friend's house.

2 Your friend is spending too much money. You advise her not to spend so much. **would**
   _____

3 We need to find satellite pictures of the solar system. We have to use the Internet. **unless**
   _____

4 You leave ice cream in the sun and it melts. **if**
   _____

5 You are invited to a party. You won't go without your best friend. **unless**
   _____

6 We use our car every day. The public transport in our area isn't efficient. **was**
   _____

8 **Say it! Talk with your partner about these situations using conditional sentences.**

Situation 1:
You heat some ice cubes. They melt.

Situation 2:
Your friend is having problems at school. She doesn't know what to do.

Situation 3:
You are daydreaming about winning a million euros.

Situation 4:
You are taking part in a competition. The winner will receive a prize.

Situation 5:
Imagine you were the mayor of your town. What changes would you introduce?

If you heat ice cubes, they melt.

If I were you, I would talk to my teacher about it.

1 Read.

If only I'd taken the car today.

Third conditional

We use the **third conditional** to talk about something that could have happened in the past, but didn't. It is used to talk about hypothetical situations or actions.
If you **had turned** on the light, you **wouldn't have fallen** over.

The *if* clause uses **if** and the **past perfect simple** and the *result* clause uses **would have** and the **past participle**.
If you **hadn't thrown away** those batteries, we **would have recycled** them.

See the list of past participles on page 159.

2 Complete the sentences with the third conditional. Use the words in brackets.

1 If you _____ *hadn't forgotten* _____ to turn off the water, the bathroom
   _____ *wouldn't have flooded* _____ . (not forget, not flood)

2 _____ the experiment if Thomas
   _____ you? (you / carry out, not help)

3 I _____ organic vegetables at the market last week if they
   _____ so expensive. (buy, not be)

4 My classmates and I _____ in the marathon if we
   _____ revise for our exams. (take part, not have to)

5 Mum _____ her clothes by hand if the washing machine
   _____ yesterday. (not wash, not break down)

6 _____ more trees if the government
   _____ them to? (the local council / plant, advise)

7 If I _____ about the job, then I
   _____ for it. (know, apply)

8 If the man _____ them the wrong directions, they
   _____ on time. (not give, arrive)

3 Complete the dialogue with the third conditional. Use the verbs in brackets.

Tom: I can't believe the local community centre has closed down.

Mary: I know. It's terrible, but even if we (1) _____'d/had tried_____ (try), we (2) _____ (not be able) to do anything.

Tom: I don't agree.

Mary: Why, what (3) _____ (you / do) if (4) _____ (you / know) it was going to close down?

Tom: Well, if somebody (5) _____ (tell) us, we (6) _____ (arrange) a gathering at the village square to come up with a plan to stop it from closing.

Mary: Anyway, the problem was the running costs. There wasn't enough money to maintain the centre. The electricity bills were too high. Maybe if we (7) _____ (save) energy, it (8) _____ (make) a difference.

Tom: You see, you agree with me. If the authorities (9) _____ (inform) us, we (10) _____ (raise) money for the centre with bring-and-buy sales and other things like that.

Mary: Mm, you're right.

Wish (for the present)

We use **wish** or **if only** and the **past simple** or the **past continuous** when a situation in the present is different to what we would like it to be.
*I **wish** I **knew** about astronomy. (But I don't know about astronomy.)*
*If only we **didn't live** in the city centre. (But we do live in the city centre.)*
*I **wish** it **wasn't raining**. (But it is raining.)*
*If only I **were relaxing** by the sea. (But I'm not relaxing by the sea.)*

We can't use **if only** in the question form. We must use **wish**.
*Do you **wish** you **were** a famous singer?*

Remember !

We can use **were** instead of **was** for the first and third person singular.
*If only it **were** hotter today!*
*I **wish** I **were** a millionaire.*

4 Complete the sentences. Use the correct form of these verbs.

> have   know   ~~live~~   not be   spend   visit

1 If only I _____lived_____ nearer to my friends in the city centre! The countryside is so boring.

2 The school children wish they _____ more about hydroelectric power.

3 Brad wishes there _____ a nuclear power station in his area.

4 If only my grandson _____ me more often.

5 I wish Dad _____ less time at the office. He's never at home!

6 Rosie wishes she _____ a better laptop.

Wish (for the past)

We use **wish** or **if only** and the **past perfect simple** or the **past perfect continuous** to say that we would like a situation in the past to have been different.
*Ivan **wishes** he **hadn't forgotten** his keys. (But he did forget them.)*
*If only they **had caught** the thief. (But they didn't catch the thief.)*
*I **wish** he **hadn't been driving** so fast. (But he was driving fast.)*

5 Look at the situations and complete the sentences. Use the words in bold.

1 Sam forgot to send me a text message and she feels bad. **forgotten**

Sam wishes she ___hadn't forgotten to send___ me a text message.

2 I spilt paint on the floor and now the head teacher wants to see me. **hadn't**

If only _____ spilt paint on the floor.

3 Celia didn't take responsibility for her actions. **had**

Celia wishes she _____ for her actions.

4 Mum didn't buy a microwave and now she regrets it. **bought**

Mum wishes _____ a microwave.

5 I didn't spend very much time on my history project. **spent**

I wish I _____ on my history project.

6 Katie didn't know how to use a projector and her presentation didn't go well. **known**

If only Katie _____ how to use a projector.

Wish + would (for the present and the future)

We use **wish/if only + would + bare infinitive**
- to talk about an annoying action someone does in the present.
  If only you **wouldn't make** such a mess in my office!
- when we want an action (not a state) to change in the future.
  Dad wishes Mandy and I would watch less television.

Note: We never use **wish/if only + would** to talk about ourselves.

6 Complete the sentences with *I wish/if only* and *would*. Use these verbs.

find	give up	not cheat	~~not forget~~	not hide	not stay

1 ___If only/I wish___ you ___wouldn't forget___ to turn off the lights every night.

2 Daniel _____ his little brother _____ his magazines.

3 Our biology teacher _____ we _____ during tests.

4 _____ our government _____ a solution to the financial crisis.

5 My parents _____ I _____ out late.

6 _____ my mum _____ smoking.

7 Circle the correct words.

1 I wish the visitors **don't throw /** **(wouldn't throw)** rubbish on the sand.

2 If only I **had won / win** first prize for the science project.

3 Sandy wishes she **didn't have to use / doesn't have to use** so much paper in the office.

4 If only my team **had scored / would score** a goal in the match yesterday evening.

5 I wish the local council **would ban / banned** cars from entering the city centre.

6 If only it **were / is** sunnier in the UK.

8 **Choose the correct answers.**

1 If these trainers _____ , everyone would have bought a pair.
   a would catch on
   b had caught on
   c caught on

2 I wish you _____ such a mess in the office every day!
   a don't make
   b hadn't made
   c wouldn't make

3 We _____ if the waves were higher.
   a would go surfing
   b could surfed
   c will have gone surfing

4 I wish we _____ to go on the school excursion next week.
   a hadn't had
   b didn't have
   c hadn't

5 More people _____ in the fire if the locals hadn't helped people escape.
   a would be injured
   b would have been injured
   c had been injured

6 If only _____ all the firewood!
   a we hadn't used up
   b we wouldn't use up
   c we haven't used up

9 **Say it! Talk with your partner about how you would like your neighbourhood to be different. Use** *I wish, if only* **and these suggestions to help you.**

- more parks
- cleaner
- not so many blocks of flats
- cycling lanes
- sports centre
- cinema complex

1 **Read.**

If we want to be healthy, we must have a balanced diet.

Conditionals with modal verbs

We can use **modal verbs** in first, second and third conditional sentences.

In first conditional sentences, we can use **can, could, will, would, should, ought to, might, must** and **needn't** and a **bare infinitive** in the *result* clause.
*If we want to be healthy, we **must have** a balanced diet.*

In second conditional sentences, we can use **could, would, should, ought to** and **might** and a **bare infinitive** in the *result* clause.
*If we lived closer to our school, we **could walk** there every morning.*

In third conditional sentences, we can use **could, would, should, ought to, might** and **needn't** and a **perfect infinitive (have + past participle)** in the *result* clause.
*I **might have come** to the adventure playground if you had invited me.*

Note: We can sometimes use **modal verbs** in the *if* clause.
*If he **can** help, call him.*

2 **Complete the sentences. Use the first or the second conditional and the words in brackets.**

1 The train ___ought to arrive___ soon unless there ___is___ a delay. (ought to, arrive, be)

2 Jennifer _____ the radio when she _____ to bed. (can, turn off, go)

3 If Harry _____ hard, he _____ the painting today. (might, try, finish)

4 As long as Katrina _____ me to the sports centre in the car this evening, you
_____ me there. (needn't, drive, walk)

5 If I _____ on an intensive course, I _____ speak Spanish before my trip
to South America. (should, go, be able to)

6 Natalie _____ music and films if she _____ a computer.
(could, download, have)

7 You _____ the plants providing it _____ . (needn't, water, rain)

8 If we _____ together, we _____ many things! (could, work, achieve)

3 Read the text and then complete the sentences using the modal verbs in brackets.

We went to Disneyland last year, but what an experience!

Our flight to Paris was delayed and we arrived at our hotel at eleven o'clock. Unfortunately, the hotel restaurant had already closed, so we couldn't have dinner. We were very hungry.

The next day, we took the bus to Disneyland. When we arrived at the gate, we couldn't go in straight away because we had forgotten our entry tickets. We had to go back to the hotel to get them! Eventually, we got into Disneyland. It was amazing! We spent all day on the rides and we really enjoyed ourselves.

At the end of the day, we decided to buy some souvenirs. But when we went to the counter to pay, my purse wasn't in my pocket. Perhaps I had lost it when we were on the rides, so my friend paid for my shopping!

Disneyland was great, but lots of things went wrong!

1 If our flight hadn't been delayed, we <u>wouldn't have arrived at our hotel at eleven o'clock</u> . (wouldn't)

2 If we had arrived at the hotel earlier, we _____ . (could)

3 If we had remembered our entry tickets, we _____ straight away. (could)

4 If we had remembered our tickets, we _____ to the hotel. (needn't)

5 If I hadn't put my purse in my pocket, I _____ lost it. (might not)

6 My friend _____ if I hadn't lost my purse. (needn't)

4 Complete the sentences with these words.

> ~~could we have seen~~   might have finished   needn't have bought
> ought to have told   shouldn't have come   you could have had

1 ____<u>Could we have seen</u>____ the stars if we had looked through the telescope?

2 If _____ any of these smartphones, which one would you have chosen?

3 We _____ our experiment if the bell hadn't rung.

4 If James had known the truth, he _____ me.

5 Anthony _____ to our garden party if he hadn't been feeling well.

6 You _____ a new dishwasher if you'd repaired the old one.

5 Circle the correct words.

1 If you like being outdoors, you (should enjoy)/ wouldn't enjoy the national park.

2 If Nadia hadn't sold her flat in central London, she **couldn't have bought / needn't have bought** her beautiful cottage.

3 If you want to exercise daily, you **should take / needn't take** the dog for a walk.

4 Danny **needn't study / must study** medicine if he doesn't want to become a doctor.

5 **Could / Ought to** you translate this document for me if I need it for my job?

6 You **could have hurt / should have hurt** yourself if you'd fallen down that hill.

6 Look at the situations and complete the sentences. Use the words in bold.

1 There may be a storm, so we should stay home. **ought**

   If there is a storm, we _____<u>ought to stay</u>_____ home.

2 It's possible that they can solve the problem. That's why they want to build a dam. **might**

   If they build a dam, they _____ the problem.

3 We don't know enough about alternative sources of energy, so we can't use them yet. **could**

   If we knew more about alternative sources of energy, we _____ them.

4 Marcus didn't hear about the protest. It's possible that he wanted to come. **may**

   Marcus _____ to the protest if he had heard about it.

5 It was possible for you to get the job. It wasn't a good idea to insult the IT manager. **might**

   If you hadn't insulted the IT manager, you _____ the job.

6 Penny may teach me how to use the machine. If she does, you don't need to help me. **needn't**

   If Penny teaches me how to use the machine, you _____ help me.

7 Say it! Talk with your partner about what advice you would give these people. Use *can, could, will, would, should, ought to, might, must* and *needn't*.

PROBLEM 1

My maths teacher always shouts at me. I'm doing the best I can, but that's not good enough.

PROBLEM 2

My parents are really strict. They don't allow me to go out with my friends.

PROBLEM 3

I only get £10 pocket money a week. That isn't enough. How can I earn some money?

PROBLEM 4

My next-door neighbour makes a lot of noise all day and even very late at night. What can I do?

If you want to earn some money, you could deliver newspapers.

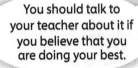

You should talk to your teacher about it if you believe that you are doing your best.

1 Read.

Gerunds

Gerunds are nouns. They are formed from verbs with the **–ing** ending.

We use **gerunds**
- as the subject of a sentence.
  Dumping *rubbish in the street is a crime.*
- as the object of a sentence.
  *I love **shopping** with my friends.*
- after prepositions.
  *My family and I are interested **in diving**.*
- after the verb **go** when we talk about activities.
  *The twins often **go climbing** at the weekend.*
- after certain verbs and phrases:

admit (to)	enjoy	like
avoid	fancy	love
be used to	feel	mention
can't help	hate	miss
can't stand	have difficulty	practise
consider	imagine	regret
deny	it's no use	risk
dislike	it's not worth	spend time
(don't) mind	keep	suggest

*I **miss spending** time with my best friend.*
*I **don't mind camping** on holidays.*
*She **can't help worrying** about her exam next week.*

Note: Certain verbs like **feel, hear, listen to, notice, see** and **watch** are followed by an object pronoun or a noun and then the gerund.

*I **felt him looking** at me.*

2 Look at the pictures and complete the sentences with gerunds formed from these verbs.

> climb   ~~exercise~~   not recycle   play   sing   walk

1 My cousin and I spend a lot of time
____exercising____ at the weekend.

2 _____ in the forest really helps
Andrew relax.

3 Natalie regrets _____ her
old magazines.

4 The boys at our school often go
_____ at the weekend.

5 Penelope is really good at
_____ the piano.

6 My grandfather listens to the birds
_____ every morning.

Full infinitive

We use the **full infinitive** after certain verbs or phrases:

afford	decide	manage	promise
agree	expect	need	refuse
allow	fail	offer	seem
appear	forget	persuade	start
arrange	hope	plan	want
ask	invite	prepare	
begin	learn	pretend	
choose	make an effort		

*We **arranged to go** to the beach after school.*

We also use the **full infinitive** after certain adjectives: **afraid, angry, anxious, ashamed, glad, happy, kind, nice, pleased, sad, sorry, stupid, surprised, upset, willing.**
*I was **surprised to hear** that you lost your mobile phone.*

Note: Certain verbs like **advise, choose, force, expect, tell** and **persuade** are followed by an object pronoun or a noun and the infinitive.
*I **persuaded my brother to lend** me his laptop.*

> **Remember!**
>
> We use the **bare infinitive** after modal verbs.
> I **should buy** a new laptop.

3 Complete the diary entry with full infinitives formed from these verbs.

ask ~~buy~~ buy give give go hear

Last week it was my birthday and it was one of the best birthdays I've ever had. My grandparents usually buy me clothes, but this year they decided (1) _____to buy_____ me something I wanted. The only thing I really wanted was a smartphone, but I was too shy (2) _____ for this. When they offered (3) _____ me money instead, I agreed.

I asked my parents for money, but Dad didn't like this idea and he refused (4) _____ me any. Instead, my parents bought me some books and clothes.

Two days later, to celebrate my birthday, my friends persuaded me (5) _____ to a charity event. We took part in a talent contest. When the time came to announce the winner of the first prize, I was surprised (6) _____ I had won, as I never win anything! The prize was a voucher from a huge electrical shop. I couldn't believe it! With this voucher, together with the money my grandparents gave me, I could afford (7) _____ the smartphone I wanted!

HAPPY BIRTHDAY

Gerunds and infinitives

Some verbs are followed by a **gerund** or a **full infinitive** without a change in meaning:
begin, bother, continue, hate, like, start
*My friends and I **love drawing**.*
*My friends and I **love to draw**.*

The following verbs are followed by a **gerund** or a **full infinitive**, but there is a change in meaning:

forget
*Julie **forgot telling** her mum about the party. (She told her mum about the party, but she doesn't remember doing it.)*
*Julie **forgot to tell** her mum about the party. (She didn't remember to tell her mum about the party.)*

go on
*Jennifer **went on playing** for hours. (She didn't stop playing.)*
*Jennifer **went on to play** with her new toy. (She stopped what she was doing and then started to play.)*

regret
*I **regret giving** Dennis my old mobile phone. (I wish that I had not given Dennis my old mobile phone.)*
*I **regret to give** you some bad news. (I feel sorry that I have to give you some bad news.)*

remember
*I **remember posting** the invitations. (I posted the invitations, and I remember doing it.)*
*I **remembered to post** the invitations. (The invitations have been posted now.)*

stop
*We **stopped eating** meat a year ago. (We don't eat meat any more.)*
*We **stopped to eat** a sandwich. (We stopped (working, walking, etc.) so that we could eat a sandwich.)*

try
Try drinking some milk before you go to bed. (Do this as an experiment because it may help you.)
*I know it's difficult, but **try to do** it. (Make an attempt, but it may not be possible.)*

4 Circle the correct words.

1 I'm afraid I don't remember **to send / sending** you this email.
2 I don't go **shopping / to shop** with my mum very often.
3 I've got a really bad headache. Please stop **to shout / shouting**.
4 My little brother regrets **to lock / locking** himself in his bedroom.
5 Henry completed a course in computer studies and went on **to study / studying** at university.
6 Tariq, remember **to turn off / turning off** your computer before you go to bed.
7 The workmen stopped **to have / having** a break because they were tired.
8 Try **to drink / drinking** some milk to help you sleep.

5 **Complete the sentences with gerunds or full infinitives. Use the verbs in brackets.**

1 The judge delayed _____announcing_____ the winner of the competition last night. (announce)

2 I don't feel like _____ to the beach this afternoon. (go)

3 I told you _____ careful, but you didn't listen to me. (be)

4 I'm sorry _____ that your grandfather is not well. (hear)

5 Robert isn't very good at _____ letters. (write)

6 My friends and I were playing in the park when it began _____ . (rain)

7 Did you notice the little boy _____ on the doorstep? (sit)

8 We regret _____ passengers that the eight o'clock train has been cancelled. (inform)

6 **Complete the second sentences so they have a similar meaning to the first sentences. Use the words in bold.**

1 It's silly to go into town because the shops close in half an hour. **worth**

It's _____not worth going_____ into town because the shops close in half an hour.

2 Nermine tries not to call her friends in Australia because phone calls are very expensive. **avoids**

Nermine _____ her friends in Australia because phone calls are very expensive.

3 His parents won't let him stay up late. **allow**

His parents won't _____ late.

4 My family and I are sad that we don't spend weekends in the country any more. **miss**

My family and I _____ in the country.

5 James said he'd help us with the shopping. **offered**

James _____ with the shopping.

6 Polly loves to take photographs of unusual buildings. **taking**

_____ of unusual buildings is something Polly loves.

7 'Why don't we go to New York for New Year?' she said. **suggested**

She _____ for New Year.

8 I enjoyed seeing my old school friends last week. **nice**

It _____ my old school friends last week.

7 **Say it! Talk with your partner about these activities. Use gerunds and infinitives.**

I love playing computer games.

I don't enjoy watching football matches.

1 Read.

Maria and Tom go jogging every day so that they stay fit. They take the dog with them in order to give him some exercise.

Clauses of purpose

We use **clauses of purpose** to explain why someone does something or why something happens. We introduce them using these words and phrases:

in order to
We use **in order to** only when the subject of the two clauses is the same. It is followed by the bare infinitive. In negative sentences, we put the word **not** before **to**.
*Borrow my camera **in order to take** photos.*
*I wrote a list **in order not to forget** anything.*

so as to
We use **so as to** only when the subject of the two clauses is the same. It is followed by the bare infinitive. In negative sentences, we put the word **not** before **to**.
*My parents go for a walk after dinner **so as to get** some exercise.*
*I didn't tell Janet everything **so as not to upset** her.*

in case
We never use **will** or **would** after **in case**, even if we are referring to the future. In this case, we use the **present simple**, the **present continuous** or the **present perfect simple**. It is followed by a noun or a subject pronoun (I, you, he, etc.) and a verb.
*I need my cash card **in case I run out of** money.*

so that
We can use **so that** when the object of the two clauses is the same or different. It is followed by a noun or a subject pronoun (I, you, he, etc.) and a verb in the **present simple** or **can/could** or **will/would**.
*John goes jogging every day **so that he stays** fit.*
*Lilly has a money box **so that she can** save money.*
*We didn't take a break **so that we would** finish early.*

for
We use a noun or an object pronoun after the word **for**.
*My mum made some fruit salad just **for me**.*

to
To is followed by the bare infinitive.
*We collected money **to buy** our teacher a present.*

2 Circle the correct words.

1 Katie got ready quickly **so that** / **for** she wouldn't be late.

2 Dee sent us a text message **so as** / **to** invite us to her party.

3 Take some extra money with you to the shopping centre **in case** / **to** you see something you like.

4 I'll take the bus home **to** / **so as not to** walk.

5 I'm leaving the office early today **so that** / **in order to** buy a new keyboard.

6 We need a table **for** / **so that** our new printer.

7 Shall we get started, **in order to** / **so as** not to waste time?

8 I'll finish my homework now **for** / **in order not to** stay up late.

3 Choose the correct answers.

1 Julian asked me to meet him after school _____ tell me a secret.

   a in order to
   b for
   c so as

2 Our teacher explains everything very clearly _____ we don't have any problems.

   a in order
   b so that
   c for

3 The children stopped talking _____ upset their teacher.

   a in order not to
   b in case
   c so as to

4 I need to buy a pump _____ inflate these balloons.

   a for
   b in order
   c to

5 Let's take some money with us _____ we go to the planetarium after school.

   a to
   b for
   c in case

6 I wrote myself a reminder _____ forget my appointment.

   a in case
   b so as not to
   c to

7 Let's buy our tickets online _____ avoid waiting in a queue.

   a so as to
   b for
   c in case

8 Mandy called the bank manager _____ a loan.

   a in order to
   b for
   c so as to

4 Complete the sentences. Use these words.

for   for   in case   in case   in order not to   so as to   so that   ~~to~~

1 Melissa wanted to go to the shopping centre _____**to**_____ meet her friends.

2 Wear your watch during the exam _____ you can check the time.

3 I stopped the celebrity _____ get her autograph.

4 Take some warm clothes with you _____ it snows.

5 We drove to a little restaurant in the country _____ lunch.

6 Julie used a calculator _____ make a mistake.

7 I'll take a hat with me _____ it's sunny.

8 I bought this cool T-shirt just _____ you.

5 **Combine the sentences using the words in brackets.**

1 I bought a book about reptiles. I want to learn more about them. (in order)

   <u>I bought a book about reptiles in order to learn more about them.</u>

2 Mum and Dad cycle to work. They want to consume less petrol. (so as to)

   _____

3 I left home early. I didn't want to be late. (in order not to)

   _____

4 Julian came to my house yesterday evening. We watched the football match together. (so that)

   _____

5 My brother and I are going into town this afternoon. We want to buy a new game. (to)

   _____

6 Sandra has to go to the electronics shop later on. She needs to fix her GPS. (so as to)

   _____

7 I'm taking my headphones to school today. We might have a lesson in the language lab. (in case)

   _____

8 Dad bought some beautiful flowers. It's Mum's birthday today. (for)

   _____

6 **Complete the advertisement. Use only one word in each blank.**

Laptop and mouse for sale

I'm selling my laptop! It's black and silver and it's only a year old. It comes with a mouse, which is also black and silver, and a black case (1) _____**to**_____ help you keep the laptop in good condition.

If you're interested, send me a text message on 6978 840 984 (2) _____ that I can contact you. Unfortunately, you can't see the laptop at the moment, as I've taken it to the local electrical shop (3) _____ a service, but leave me your number in (4) _____ for me to send you a photo.

Just in (5) _____ you're wondering why I want to sell the laptop, I'm selling it so (6) _____ to buy an even newer one!

---

7 **Say it!** Imagine you are going on a hike in the mountains with your friends. Talk with your partner about what you would take with you and why. Use these ideas to help you.

- compass
- mosquito repellent
- mobile phone
- sun cream
- map

- plenty of water
- first aid kit
- hat
- sandwiches
- whistle

I'd take a hat so as not get sunstroke.

I'd take a whistle in case I got lost.

1   Read.

Alan's having his car washed.

The causative

We use the **causative** to talk about something
- that someone does for us.
  I'm having my photos developed.
- unpleasant that happened to us that we didn't want to happen.
  Harry had his laptop stolen last night.

We form the **causative** with the verb **have** + object + past participle of the main verb.
John has his clothes ironed.

See the list of past participles on page 159.

We can use **by + agent** to show who does the action.
The Adams family had their house redecorated by an interior designer.

Note: When we are speaking, we can use the verb **get** instead of **have**.
However, when we talk about unpleasant events, we must use **have**.
We're getting a new home cinema delivered this evening.
Our neighbours had their car stolen last week.

Present simple	*I have my car washed.*
Present continuous	*I'm having my car washed.*
Past simple	*I had my car washed.*
Past continuous	*I was having my car washed.*
Present perfect simple	*I've had my car washed.*
Present perfect continuous	*I've been having my car washed.*
Past perfect simple	*I had had my car washed.*
Past perfect continuous	*I'd been having my car washed.*
Future simple	*I'll have my car washed.*
Future continuous	*I'll be having my car washed.*
Future perfect simple	*I'll have had my car washed.*
be going to	*I'm going to have my car washed.*
modals (present)	*I must have my car washed.*
modals (past)	*I should have had my car washed.*

Remember !

The object of a causative sentence must appear before the past participle of the main verb.
I've had **my computer upgraded**.

2 Complete the sentences with the causative. Use the correct present tense and the words in brackets.

1   I _'m/am having my new printer delivered_ this afternoon. (my new printer / deliver)

2   Toby's hair grows very fast. He _____ every month. (his hair / cut)

3   Do the children _____ ? (their rooms / tidy)

4   We _____ now because it's raining. (our windows / not clean)

5   Does Mrs Dawson _____ every week? (her house / clean)

6   Next month, we _____ . (our home cinema / fix)

7   They _____ any more. (the newspaper / not deliver)

8   At the moment, my classmates and I _____ . (our new uniforms / fit)

3 Complete the sentences with the causative. Use the correct past or future tense and these verbs.

> cut   develop   make   not deliver   paint   publish   steal   water

1   Last night, my neighbours _____ had _____ their TV _____ stolen _____ .

2   We _____ our garden _____ by Stan for years before he retired.

3   The award-winning author _____ her new book _____ a week ago.

4   Before the photo studio closed last night, I _____ my photos _____ .

5   This time tomorrow, Julie _____ her hair _____ at the hairdresser's.

6   I _____ my car _____ red yesterday.

7   The children _____ their new furniture _____ at eleven o'clock this morning.

8   I _____ my new curtains _____ by John soon.

4 Read the dialogues and complete the sentences using the causative form.

1   **A:** Oh, your kitchen looks lovely! Did you paint it yourself, Martha?

     B: No, I didn't. I _____ had my kitchen/it painted _____ by a professional decorator.

2   **A:** Are you going to iron those shirts yourself?

     B: No, I'm not. I _____ by Mum.

3   **A:** Do you go shopping at the supermarket every week?

     B: No, I never go shopping at the supermarket. I go online, place my order and _____ to my home.

4   **A:** Henry's garden is so big. It must take him ages to do the gardening.

     B: He doesn't do it himself. He _____ for him for years.

5   **A:** Is Jennifer making your wedding cake for you?

     B: No, she isn't. We _____ by the Delicious Cake Company.

6   **A:** Has your computer been repaired now?

     B: Yes, but it cost a lot of money. I _____ before I realised that the local shop could have done it more cheaply.

7   **A:** What happened to your phone?

     B: I _____ last night. Someone must have taken it from my bag when I wasn't looking. Now I have to buy a new one.

8   **A:** Is that a new car?

     B: No, I've had this car for a while, but I just _____ at the garage this morning, so it looks new!

5 **Rewrite the sentences using the words given. Use between two and five words.**

1 Toby often washes Veronica's car. **has**

   Veronica _____*often has her car washed*_____ by Toby.

2 Our general manager has arranged for her office to be furnished next week. **having**

   Our general manager _____ next week.

3 The technician has set up a wireless internet connection. **had**

   We _____ wireless internet connection set up.

4 I must arrange for the rubbish to be collected. **have**

   I _____ collected.

5 Helen is going to arrange for somebody to build her a new cupboard. **built**

   Helen is going to _____ .

6 A gardener planted some flowers for me yesterday. **planted**

   I _____ by a gardener yesterday.

7 A cleaner was cleaning my house all day yesterday. **cleaned**

   I _____ all day yesterday.

8 Cathy should have arranged for somebody to water the garden. **had**

   Cathy should _____ .

9 A famous fashion designer will design a dress for Gabriella. **will**

   Gabriella _____ by a famous fashion designer.

10 Tommy was in pain after the dentist pulled out his tooth. **had**

   Tommy _____ out by the dentist.

6 **Say it! Talk with your partner about what Nellie is dreaming. Use the causative and these suggestions.**

- do homework / teacher
- tidy room / brother
- walk my dog / sister
- carry my school bag / friend
- wash my hair / hairdresser
- make meals / famous chef

I'm having my homework done by my teacher.

I'm having my room tidied by my brother.

1 **Complete the sentences. Use the words in brackets.**

1 If you _____press_____ this button, the computer will turn off. (press)

2 Dan _____ his cash card unless he runs out of money. (not use)

3 _____ slippery if it rains? (this road / be)

4 If I cycled to school, it _____ me 15 minutes. (take)

5 _____ if you kept it away from the sunlight? (this plant / grow)

6 We _____ late if we hadn't missed the bus. (not arrive)

2 **Look at these situations and write conditional sentences.**

1 Jeremy dropped his monitor and it broke. He needed to buy a new one.
   If Jeremy hadn't dropped/broken his monitor, he wouldn't have needed to buy a new one.

2 The sink is full of dishes, but I don't have time to wash them.
   _____

3 Your friend has asked you for some advice. Her parents are upset with her because she lied to them. You think she should apologise.
   _____

4 Robbie and his mum are shopping. He wants a new computer game, but his mum doesn't buy it for him because she thinks it's very expensive.
   _____

5 Judy left her keys at her friend's house. She couldn't open her front door.
   _____

6 A teacher is telling her students that they'll go on an excursion providing their test results are good.
   _____

3 **Circle the correct words.**

1 It's very hot today! I wish I **had brought** / **brought** some sun cream with me.

2 The train ride last night was so boring. If only I **took / had taken** my MP4 player with me.

3 I'm trying to sleep, but the dogs keep making a noise. I wish they **would stop / had stopped** barking.

4 Colette won second prize in the diving competition. She wishes she **came / had come** first.

5 This dress costs £150! I wish it **weren't / isn't** so expensive.

6 I'm expecting a call for a new job. If only the phone **would ring / had rung**!

7 Everyone said that the school trip was a lot of fun. I wish I **went / had gone**!

8 It's such a sunny day. If only I **didn't have to / wouldn't have to** study!

4 Choose the correct answers.

1 If the fire brigade had arrived earlier, the building _____ .
   a wouldn't burn down
   (b) wouldn't have burnt down
   c would burn down

2 Unless we service the air-conditioning unit, we _____ .
   a hadn't turned it on
   b didn't turn it on
   c shouldn't turn it on

3 If I _____ where your mobile phone was, I would tell you.
   a know
   b had known
   c knew

4 As long as your brother _____ with you, you can go to the party.
   a goes
   b will go
   c went

5 What a noise! I wish you _____ your electric guitar in the middle of the night.
   a hadn't played
   b don't play
   c wouldn't play

5 Complete the text with gerunds or full infinitives. Use the verbs in brackets.

A month ago, our school decided (1) _to take part_ (take part) in a competition. The aim was for students from all the schools in our area to prepare a presentation called *The future of our environment through the eyes of the youth of today*.

My three classmates and I agreed (2) _____ (prepare) a presentation and for two weeks, we spent time (3) _____ (look) for information and photos on the Internet.

When the day of the competition arrived, we all gathered at the school. My classmates and I weren't willing (4) _____ (go) first, so we watched the others. Their presentations were so professional, like something Dad would prepare. Our turn came and even though I can't stand (5) _____ (speak) in front of an audience, I did. Our presentation wasn't as amazing as the others, but we managed (6) _____ (express) our opinion and we felt happy.

My classmates and I were very surprised (7) _____ (hear) that we had won. Even though my friends told me not to, I couldn't help (8) _____ (ask) the judges how they had come to their final decision. 'It was easy,' the judge told me. 'It was obvious you had spent time (9) _____ (prepare) your presentation and you managed (10) _____ (get) your points across very well, so well done!'

6 Combine the sentences using the words in bold.

1 Mark is going to study medicine. He wants to become a doctor. **in order to**
   Mark is going to study medicine in order to become a doctor.

2 Don't hang out the washing. It might rain. **in case**
   _____

3 Helen turned on the heating. She felt cold. **so as not to**
   _____

4 The museum is closed to visitors. It is being renovated. **for**
   _____

5 Susie picked up the watering can. She wanted to water the plants. **to**
   _____

6 I'm saving my pocket money. I want to buy a new computer. **in order to**
   _____

7 Complete the sentences with the causative. Use the words in brackets.

1   At the moment, I _'m/am having my digital camera repaired_ . (digital camera / repair)

2   My parents usually _____ once a week. (house / clean)

3   The author was very disappointed that _____ .
    (her new book / not publish)

4   _____ we _____
    tomorrow? (our teeth / clean)

5   I believe the school _____ very soon. (new library / build)

6   Our head teacher _____ tomorrow afternoon. (a solar panel / install)

7   Theresa always _____ to her house on Friday evening. (pizza / deliver)

8   Mum _____ last week. (the ironing / not do)

9   Nabil _____ for him before he learnt how to cook. (his meals / cook)

10 _____ you _____ when you
    lived at home? (your clothes / iron)

WRITING PROJECT

8 Look at a project about an environmentally friendly structure. Circle the correct words.

London

If you (1) **take** / **took** a walk around London, you'll see this very impressive and unusual architectural structure. It's London's first environmentally friendly skyscraper. It is called the 'Swiss Re Tower' as the Swiss Reinsurance Company (2) **had it constructed / had constructed it**.

It is 180 metres tall and there are 40 floors. It is also known as 'The Gherkin' because it looks like a gherkin. The building is covered in glass, (3) **in order to / for** allow natural light and ventilation, (4) **so that / so as to** energy consumption can be reduced. In summer, warm air is removed from the building, and in winter, solar heating is used to warm the building. Moreover, natural light passes through the building (5) **so that / for** a more pleasant working environment. At the same time, the cost of lighting is very low. In fact, if we (6) **compare / compared** its consumption to that of a regular building, we'd see that it is actually 50% less.

The Swiss Re Tower is certainly out of the ordinary, but it is surprising (7) **to hear / hearing** that many Londoners wish such a building (8) **hadn't been built / wasn't built** in the centre of the City of London.

9 Now it's your turn to do a project about an environmentally friendly structure. Find or draw a picture of the building and write about it.

1 Read.

He said that she didn't get the promotion she wanted.

Reported speech: statements

We use **reported speech** to tell someone what another person has said.

When we report something, we change the tense to a tense further back in the past as follows:

Direct speech

Present simple
'Ella **works** in tourism,' Tom said.

Present continuous
'Ella **is working** in tourism,' Tom said.

Present perfect simple
'Ella **has worked** in tourism,' Tom said.

Present perfect continuous
'Ella **has been working** in tourism,' Tom said.

Past simple
'Ella **worked** in tourism,' Tom said.

Past continuous
'Ella **was working** in tourism,' Tom said.

Future simple (will)
'Ella **will work** in tourism,' Tom said.

be going to
'Ella **is going to** work in tourism,' Tom said.

can
'Ella **can work** in tourism,' Tom said.

must
'Ella **must work** every day,' Tom said.

may
'Ella **may work** in tourism,' Tom said.

Reported speech

Past simple
Tom said (that) Ella **worked** in tourism.

Past continuous
Tom said (that) Ella **was working** in tourism.

Past perfect simple
Tom said (that) Ella **had worked** in tourism.

Past perfect continuous
Tom said (that) Ella **had been working** in tourism.

Past perfect simple
Tom said (that) Ella **had worked** in tourism.

Past perfect continuous
Tom said (that) Ella **had been working** in tourism.

would
Tom said (that) Ella **would work** in tourism.

was going to
Tom said (that) Ella **was going to** work in tourism.

could
Tom said (that) Ella **could work** in tourism.

had to
Tom said (that) Ella **had to work** every day.

might
Tom said (that) Ella **might work** in tourism.

Reported speech: statements

In **reported speech**, we also change personal pronouns (**I, you, he, she, it, we, you, they**), possessive adjectives (**my, your, his, her, its, our, your, their**), possessive pronouns (**mine, yours, his, hers, ours, yours, theirs**) and object pronouns (**me, you, him, her, it, us, you, them**).

'I found my keys,' Alice said.
Alice said **she had found her** keys.
'Melanie made me a chocolate milkshake,' Michael said.
Michael said Melanie **had made him** a chocolate milkshake.

We can use the word **that** after **he/she,** etc. **said** and **he/she,** etc. **told me/them,** etc.
'I've been sending emails,' **she said.**
She said (that) she had been sending emails.

Note: We do not need to change tenses when we are talking about something that is still true.
'My brother lives in Finland,' Julie said.
Julie said that her brother lives in Finland. (It is still true that her brother lives in Finland.)

There is also no tense change when the reporting verb is in the present. We also don't change the tense when we are talking about a law of science and with the following: **past perfect simple, past perfect continuous,** second and third conditional sentences, **would, could, might, should, ought to, used to, had better, mustn't** and **must** when it is used to express deduction.

'Eating too many sweets is bad for our health,' **says** Mum.
Mum says eating too many sweets **is** bad for our health.
'The sun rises in the east,' said Mr White.
Mr White said (that) the sun **rises** in the east.
'You should retrain as a teacher,' Mum told Dad.
Mum told Dad that he **should retrain** as a teacher.

> **Remember !**
>
> When we use **tell** with reported speech it is followed by an object, whereas **say** is not followed by an object.
> John **told me** (that) Reem was doing a writing course.
> John **said** (that) Reem was doing a writing course.

2 Complete the sentences in reported speech.

1 'We spent a lot of time in Morocco,' Monica said.

Monica said _____(that) they had spent_____ a lot of time in Morocco.

2 'Our department isn't going to hire any more people,' the manager said.

The manager said _____ any more people.

3 'I've decided to do a teacher-training course,' Jennifer said.

Jennifer said _____ a teacher-training course.

4 'The jacket may not be leather,' Dad said.

Dad said _____ leather.

5 'Serena wants to start job hunting,' Chris said.

Chris said _____ job hunting.

6 'I'll email the applicant,' the secretary told me.

The secretary told me _____ the applicant.

7 'We were waiting for the courier,' Mum and Dad said.

Mum and Dad said _____ for the courier.

8 'John handed in his assignment on time,' said Mr Brown.

Mr Brown said _____ his assignment on time.

3 Complete the dialogues using reported speech. Use the words in brackets.

1 **Vicky:** I'm getting ready for my graduation ceremony. (a party)
   Ross: Oh. I thought you said _____ *you were getting ready for a party* _____ .

2 **Harriet:** Lucy's been working in an estate agency for ten years. (five years)
   Lee: Oh. I thought she said _____ .

3 **Miss Clarkson:** I'll get us both some coffee. (tea)
   Clare: Oh. I thought you said _____ .

4 **Alice:** Dina applied for a university grant. (a small business grant)
   Gina: Oh. I thought she said _____ .

5 **Dan:** Jane and Tim were working in a factory when it closed down. (museum)
   Joe: Oh. I thought they said _____ .

6 **Felicity:** I always send my reports on Thursdays. (Tuesdays)
   Henry: Oh. I thought you said _____ .

7 **Duncan:** Kevin can't find Mr Smith's office. (Mrs Smith's office)
   James: Oh. I thought he said _____ .

8 **Penny:** You must get your application in by the 15th March. (15th April)
   Liam: Oh. I thought you said _____ .

4 Rewrite the sentences in direct speech.

1 Robbie said that he'd been speaking to an economist all morning.
   _____ *'I've been speaking to an economist all morning.'* _____ Robbie said.

2 My parents told me that I shouldn't come home later than midnight.
   _____ my parents told me.

3 Oliver said that he had never been to a planetarium before.
   _____ Oliver said.

4 Tina said that she was going to be made redundant.
   _____ Tina said.

5 Elizabeth said that she works long hours.
   _____ Elizabeth said.

6 Tamara said that she was working on a company project.
   _____ Tamara said.

Changes in time and place

When we use **reported speech**, besides the changes in tenses, personal and possessive pronouns, there are other changes which need to be made to words and phrases that talk about time and place.

today	*that day*
tonight	*that night*
tomorrow	*the following day/the next day*
yesterday	*the day before/the previous day*
last year	*the year before/the previous year*
next week	*the week after/the following week*
a month ago	*the month before/the previous month*
now	*then*
ago	*before*
at the moment	*at that moment*
here	*there*
this/these	*that/those*

'I got a bonus **yesterday**,' Tim said.
Tim said that he had got a bonus **the day before**.

'The graduate is being interviewed **at the moment**,' Celia said.
Celia said that the graduate was being interviewed **at that moment**.

5 **Circle the correct words.**

1 Our headteacher said that we had to look smart for the graduation ceremony **tomorrow / the following** day.

2 The applicant said that she had trained to be a chef **the year before / last year**.

3 Frank told his wife that he would be home early **that / this** evening.

4 Three days ago, the singer said he was going to sign some autographs for his fans **tomorrow / the following** morning.

5 Last week, Catherine said that she had worked overtime **yesterday / the day before**.

6 Mum told us that we had to economise **this / that** summer.

7 You said that you had put the money **here / there**.

8 Last Saturday, Richard told us that he would visit us **tonight / that night**.

6 **Rewrite the sentences in reported speech.**

1 'I'm going for a job interview tomorrow,' Mandy said.
   Mandy said (that) she was going for a job interview the next day/the following day.

2 'We walked around Central Park last week,' Keeley told me.
   _____

3 'The technician is fixing my laptop at the moment,' Luke said.
   _____

4 'My colleagues are going to go out for dinner tonight,' Lynne said.
   _____

5 'We're flying to the States next month,' my boss said.
   _____

6 'There was a huge recession last year,' the accountant said.
   _____

7 'I'm sure I put my keys here,' Mum said.
   _____

8 'Lisa didn't make this mess on the floor,' said Tina.
   _____

7 **Say it! Look at these messages and tell your partner what these people said.**

1 I had a great day yesterday. I visited a friend and we watched a film.
FROM FRANK

2 I'm not enjoying this presentation. It's boring and I want to leave.
FROM BETH

3 Faye and I will be relaxing by the sea tomorrow. I can't wait!
FROM DAN

4 We must hand in our assignments next Monday.
FROM CELIA

5 I can't come tonight because I must study.
FROM TOM

Frank said that he had had a great day the day before.

Frank also said that he had visited a friend and that they had watched a film.

1 Read.

James visited his dad at his office. He asked his dad what building he was working on.

Reported questions

We usually use the verb **ask** to report questions. We often use an object with **ask**.
'Can I have an apple?' Jodie **asked me**.
Jodie **asked me** if/whether she could have an apple.

Questions with question words

We use the same **question word** that is in the **direct question**.

> **Remember!**
>
> The changes that apply to **reported statements** also apply to **reported questions**.

Direct speech	**Reported speech**
Present simple	**Past simple**
'Whose is this bag?' he asked.	He asked **whose** that bag **was**.
Present continuous	**Past continuous**
'What is the boy drawing?' asked Mrs Jones.	Mrs Jones asked **what** the boy **was drawing**.
Present perfect simple	**Past perfect simple**
'Who has the teacher chosen?' she asked.	She asked **who** the teacher **had chosen**.
Present perfect continuous	**Past perfect continuous**
'Who has been making so much noise?' Jo asked.	Jo asked **who had been making** so much noise.
Past simple	**Past perfect simple**
'Where did you find that ring?' she asked.	She asked **where** I **had found** that ring.
Past continuous	**Past perfect continuous**
'Why was the baby crying?' Dad asked.	Dad asked **why** the baby **had been crying**.
will	**would**
'When will you go to the bank?' Mum asked.	Mum asked **when** I **would go** to the bank.
can	**could**
'How high can you jump?' Mr Lee asked.	Mr Lee asked me **how** high I **could jump**.
must	**had to**
'Which cough syrup must I take?' Dad asked.	Dad asked **which** cough syrup he **had to take**.

2 **Look at the pictures and complete the reported questions.**

1 The teacher asked
   <u>who was going to tell her the answer</u> .

2 The manager asked
   _____ .

3 The employee asked
   _____ .

4 The passenger asked
   _____ .

5 The boy asked _____ .

6 Harry asked his brother
   _____ .

Questions without question words

When a **direct question** doesn't start with **a question word**, we form the **reported question** with the word **if**. We can also use **whether**.

Direct speech

Present simple
*'**Do** you **like** peanut butter?' Tim asked.*

Present continuous
*'**Are** they **playing** together?' he asked.*

Past simple
*'**Did** you **have** lunch?' she asked.*

Past continuous
*'**Were** you **playing** with Ted?' she asked.*

Present perfect simple
*'**Have** they **finished**?' she asked.*

Present perfect continuous
*'**Have** you **been exercising**?' he asked.*

will
*'**Will** you **answer** the phone, please?' Mum asked.*
*'**Are** you **going to** help me, George?' I said.*

can
*'**Can** I **bring** a friend to the party?' the man asked.*

must
*'**Must** I **drink** all the milk?' Kelly asked.*

Reported speech

Past simple
*Tim asked **if/whether** I **liked peanut butter**.*

Past continuous
*He asked **if/whether** they **were playing** together.*

Past perfect simple
*She asked **if/whether** I **had had** lunch.*

Past perfect continuous
*She asked **if/whether** I **had been playing** with Ted.*

Past perfect simple
*She asked **if/whether** they **had finished**.*

Past perfect continuous
*He asked **if/whether** we **had been exercising**.*

would
*Mum asked **if/whether** I **would answer** the phone.*
*I asked **if/whether** George **was going to** help me.*

could
*The man asked **if/whether** he **could bring** a friend to the party.*

had to
*Kelly asked **if/whether** she **had to drink** all the milk.*

3 **Circle the correct words.**

1 Sandra asked **if I lived** / **did I live** in the city centre.

2 My brother asked me **whether I had eaten** / **did I eat** a whole pizza the night before.

3 The receptionist asked **were we going to check out** / **if we were going to check out** that morning.

4 Angela asked the history teacher **does she have to** / **whether she had to** learn the text off by heart.

5 William asked me if **did I study** / **I had been studying** botany for long.

6 Tony asked whether **if he could write** / **he could write** about wildlife for his school project.

7 The teacher asked us if **we had finished** / **whether we have finished** the test.

8 Mum asked me **if I liked** / **do I like** her new dress.

4 Read the job interview and complete the sentences using reported speech. Only report the words in bold.

Mr Oliver: Good morning, Josh. My name is Mr Oliver. I'm the Human Resources Manager.

Josh: Good morning, Mr Oliver.

Mr Oliver: Josh, **why do you want to work in the film industry?**

Josh: Because my degree is in media studies, and it's my dream to be a film producer.

Mr Oliver: I see. **What work experience do you have?**

Josh: **I've been working for a local production company for six years.**

Mr Oliver: **Why did you decide to look for another job?**

Josh: **I want to advance my career,** to work in a larger company.

Mr Oliver: I see. Now, **do you speak any foreign languages?**

Josh: Yes, I speak French and Spanish.

Mr Oliver: And **when can you start working for us?**

Josh: **I need to give my current boss a month's notice.** Then, I can start.

Mr Oliver: Thank you, Josh. **I'll contact you at the beginning of next week.**

Josh: Thank you, Mr Oliver. **I'll be expecting your call.**

1 Mr Oliver asked Josh _why he wanted to work in the film industry_
  _____ .

2 Mr Oliver asked Josh _____
  _____ .

3 Josh said (that) _____
  _____ .

4 Mr Oliver asked Josh _____
  _____ .

5 Josh said (that) _____
  _____ .

6 Mr Oliver asked Josh _____
  _____ .

7 Mr Oliver asked Josh _____
  _____ .

8 Josh said (that) _____
  _____ .

9 Mr Oliver said (that) _____
  _____ .

10 Josh said (that) _____
  _____ .

Reported commands and requests

Commands

Reported commands are usually introduced with the verb **tell**. **Tell** is followed by an object and the full infinitive. When the command is negative, we put **not** before the full infinitive.

*'**Post** these letters as soon as possible,' my supervisor said.*
*My supervisor **told me to post** those letters as soon as possible.*
*'**Don't spend** all your money,' Dad said.*
*Dad **told me not to spend** all my money.*

Requests

Reported requests are usually introduced with the verb **ask**. **Ask** is followed by an object and the full infinitive. When the request is negative, we put **not** before the full infinitive. Note that we leave out the word **please** in reported requests.

*'Please **come** along to the meeting,' Rosanne said.*
*Rosanne **asked me to come** along to the meeting.*
*'Please **don't make** a lot of noise,' the teacher said.*
*The teacher **asked us not to make** a lot of noise.*

> **Remember !**
>
> The changes that apply to **reported statements** also apply to **reported commands** and **reported requests**.

---

5 **Write what the people said in reported speech.**

Find out if there are any vacancies in the fast food restaurant.

1 John told me <u>to find out if there were</u> any vacancies in the fast food restaurant.

Make an appointment with the careers advisor.

2 Aunt Helen told Ron _____ an appointment with the careers advisor.

Please make an effort to do well in the test.

3 Mum asked me _____ to do well in the test.

Postpone the match until tomorrow.

4 Our coach told us _____ _____ .

Don't mention the price of this present to Mum.

5 My sister told me _____ _____ .

Please don't forget to call the estate agency.

6 The boss asked her secretary _____ .

Please don't turn on the printer.

7 Mrs Wallace asked the secretary _____ .

Don't call me by my nickname.

8 Joe told his parents _____ _____ .

6 **Choose the correct answers.**

1 Ben asked me whether _____ to school that morning.

   (a) I could drive him
   b to drive him
   c please drive him

2 I asked my swimming instructor _____ last year's record.

   a if it had broken
   b who had broken
   c to have broken

3 Jamila told me _____ an application letter to the advertising company.

   a whether to not send
   b don't send
   c not to send

4 My manager asked me _____ the presentation by the following week.

   a to finish
   b if I can finish
   c finish

5 Hana asked her husband _____ so many bags in the kitchen.

   a why there were
   b if there are
   c why were there

6 Eliza asked _____ our homework the following morning.

   a to hand in
   b whether we had to hand in
   c do we have to hand in

7 The twins asked their parents _____ their room that morning.

   a if they had to tidy
   b whether they have to tidy
   c do we have to tidy

8 The police officer told the cyclist _____ in the cycling lane.

   a stay
   b don't stay
   c to stay

7 **Say it! Imagine that you went for an interview for a summer job teaching English and you got the job. Talk with your partner about what questions the interviewer asked you and what he/she told you to do and not to do when teaching. Use these ideas to help you.**

- Why are you interested in the job?
- Do you have any hobbies?
- How long can you work for?
- Where do you live?
- Do you enjoy working with children?
- Have you ever taught English before?
- Do you speak any foreign languages?
- Can you tell me how you would teach grammar, please?
- Can you explain how you would deal with difficult students, please?
- Tell students to ask questions if they don't understand.
- Tell students to revise vocabulary every day.
- Don't let students eat during the lesson.
- Don't allow students to hand in their work late.

The interviewer asked me why I was interested in the job.

She asked me if I had any hobbies.

1 **Read.**

She promised that she would help more around the house.

She refused to tidy her room.

Reporting verbs

The most common reporting verbs are **say** and **tell** for statements, **tell** for commands, and **ask** for questions and requests. However, there are other reporting verbs that we can use to report what a person said more accurately.

Verb + full infinitive

agree	'Yes, I'll come with you,' he said.	He **agreed to come** with me.
offer	'Shall I get you a drink?' he asked.	He **offered to get** me a drink.
promise	'I promise I won't be late,' he said.	He **promised not to be** late.
refuse	'No, I won't give you the ball,' he said.	He **refused to give** me the ball.
threaten	'Stop fighting or I'll punish you,' he said.	He **threatened to punish** me if I didn't stop fighting.

Verb + object + full infinitive

advise	'You should eat more fruit,' he said.	He **advised me to eat** more fruit.
ask	'Could you answer the phone?' he said.	He **asked me to answer** the phone.
beg	'Please, please tell me,' he said.	He **begged me to tell** him.
command	'Stand to attention,' he said.	He **commanded them to stand** to attention.
invite	'Will you come over for dinner?' he said.	He **invited me to come over** for dinner.
order	'Go to the head teacher's office,' he said.	He **ordered me to go** to the head teacher's office.
persuade	'Can you clean my room for me, please?' he said.	He **persuaded me to clean** his room.
remind	'Don't forget to take some money,' he said.	He **reminded me to take** some money.
warn	'Don't stand near the edge,' he said.	He **warned me not to stand** near the edge.

Reporting verbs

Verb (+ preposition) + gerund

admit (to)	'Yes, I broke the glass,' he said.	He **admitted (to) breaking** the glass.
accuse (sb of)	'You took my pen,' he said.	He **accused me of taking** his pen.
apologise for	'I'm sorry I didn't tell you the truth,' he said.	He **apologised for not telling** me the truth.
boast about	'I've got a faster car than you,' he said.	He **boasted about having** a faster car than me.
deny	'I didn't damage your bike,' he said.	He **denied damaging** my bike.
insist on	'You must go with me,' he said.	He **insisted on me going** with him.
suggest	'Let's have a break,' he said.	He **suggested having** a break.

Verbs + that

announce	'I'm going backpacking,' he said.	He **announced that** he was going backpacking.
complain	'You are always late,' he said.	He **complained that** I was always late.
deny	'I didn't scratch the car,' he said.	He **denied that** he had scratched the car.
exclaim/remark	'What a beautiful painting,' he said.	He **exclaimed/remarked that** it was a beautiful painting.
explain	'I took the pen by mistake,' he said.	He **explained that** he had taken the pen by mistake.
promise	'I promise I'll be good,' he said.	He **promised that** he would be good.
protest	'I don't want to go to bed now,' he said.	He **protested that** he didn't want to go to bed then.
suggest	'You ought to get some rest,' he said.	He **suggested that** I (should) get some rest.

2 **Complete the sentences. Use these words.**

> accuse   apologise   ~~boast~~   complain   explain   offer   refuse   warn

1 'I got 100% for the French test,' said Carrie.

Carrie _____**boasted**_____ about getting 100% for the French test.

2 'Don't be late for work again,' my supervisor said.

My supervisor _____ me not to be late for work again.

3 'John, you broke the printer!' said the secretary.

The secretary _____ John of breaking the printer.

4 'I'll drive you to the theatre,' said Mum.

Mum _____ to drive me to the theatre.

5 'I'm sorry I broke the mirror,' said the removal man.

The removal man _____ for breaking the mirror.

6 'You never want to go anywhere,' my sister said.

My sister _____ that I never wanted to go anywhere.

7 'No, I don't want to wear this hat,' said Wendy.

Wendy _____ to wear that hat.

8 'I thought Kate wanted me to tell the teacher,' said Jake.

Jake _____ that he had thought Kate had wanted him to tell the teacher.

3 **Circle the correct words.**

1 My sister agreed **(to help)** / **helping** me with my project.

2 Cathy begged **not to tell** / **me not to tell** her secret.

3 Peter denied **that he had lost** / **to lose** the keys.

4 Mel suggested **having** / **to have** a swim.

5 I promise **that I'm not** / **not to be** impolite again.

6 Jack invited **us to come** / **that we come** to his party.

4 **Complete the sentences in reported speech.**

1 'Don't forget to wear a suit for the interview,' Hannah said to her sister.
   Hannah reminded her sister _____ to wear a suit _____ for the interview.

2 'I didn't leave all these plates in the sink,' Julie said.
   Julie denied _____ in the sink.

3 'I'll buy you some new summer clothes,' Mum said to me.
   Mum promised that _____ some new summer clothes.

4 'Let's call an electrician to install these new light bulbs,' Anna told her Dad.
   Anna suggested _____ those new light bulbs.

5 'Put the phone down or I'll call the boss,' Mark said.
   Mark threatened _____ if I didn't put the phone down.

6 'I'm sorry, but I won't change my mind,' Jake said.
   Jake refused _____ his mind.

7 'You ought to put away your things,' my sister said.
   My sister suggested _____ my things.

8 'We must invite our neighbours to the party,' said Dad.
   Dad insisted on _____ to the party.

5 **Rewrite the sentences in bold in reported speech. Use these verbs.**

advise   agree   apologise   ~~ask~~   exclaim   insist on   invite   warn

Last week, my kitchen suddenly flooded. I called the plumber, but he was busy. I called again and said, (1) **'Please come to my house** today. It's urgent.'

The plumber said, 'OK, (2) **I'll be there soon,**' and he arrived a couple of hours later. Unfortunately, he wasn't able to fix the tap. He said to me, (3) **'You shouldn't touch the tap until it's fixed.** I'll come back tomorrow.'

As I couldn't cook anything, I decided to order pizza. I didn't want to eat alone, so I called my friend and said, (4) **'Come and have lunch at my house** today.' A little later, after we had eaten, my friend wanted a glass of water. I said to her, (5) **'Don't touch the tap.** The plumber is coming to fix it tomorrow.' She didn't pay attention and she turned on the tap. Suddenly, there was a loud noise and the pipes burst. I looked at her in shock.

She said to me, (6) **'I'm sorry I didn't listen to you.'** I didn't know what to do; there was water everywhere. She said to me, (7) **'I must help you clean up,'** so we got a couple of mops and got to work. I was so upset and I said, (8) **'What a disastrous day!'**

1 I asked the plumber/him to come to my house.
2 _____
3 _____
4 _____
5 _____
6 _____
7 _____
8 _____

6 Rewrite the sentences using the reporting verbs in bold.

1 'I'm going to hand in my resignation,' my colleague said. **announce**
   <u>My colleague announced that he/she was going to hand in his/her resignation.</u>

2 'There isn't any air conditioning in this building,' the employees said. **complain**
   _____

3 'We'll stay until the film finishes,' Tara said. **insist**
   _____

4 'What a boring job!' Josh said. **remark**
   _____

5 'You have to finish your CV before you start applying for jobs,' my uncle said. **explained**
   _____

6 'Put the bag down,' the police officer said to the man. **ordered**
   _____

7 'What a tasty burger,' said Johnny. **exclaim**
   _____

8 'Please, please help me,' the little boy said to the lady. **beg**
   _____

7 Say it! Look at the pictures and what the people are saying. Then report what they said to your partner using the reporting verbs given.

1 I'm sorry I deleted your email. **apologise**

2 Don't forget to look at my presentation. **remind**

3 I got a huge bonus! **announce**

4 Don't miss another history lesson. **warn**

5 I'll lend you my phone at the weekend. **promise**

6 I didn't take your laptop. **deny**

7 I'll drive you to school. **offer**

8 It's so cold in here. **complain that**

He apologised for deleting my email.

My mum offered to drive me to school.

1 Read.

The roads have been closed due to heavy snow.

Passive voice: present, past and future

We use the **passive voice** when
- we want to emphasise the action rather than who does it.
  *A new aquarium **is being built** in the city centre.*
- when we don't know who does the action.
  *The jewellery **was stolen** from the safe.*
- when it's obvious who does the action.
  *Many people **were helped** out of the burning building. (by the firemen)*

We form the **passive voice** with the auxiliary verb **be** in the same tense as the main verb in the active sentence and the past participle of the main verb. The object of the active sentence becomes the subject of the passive sentence. We use **by** if we want to say who or what (**the agent**) does the action.
*My friends **gave** me a lot of presents for my graduation. (active sentence)*
*I **was given** a lot of presents **by** my friends for my graduation. (passive sentence)*

See the list of past participles on page 159.

The verb **let** is used in active sentences, but the verb **allow** is used in passive sentences.
*They **let** us take pictures of the aircraft. (active sentence)*
*We **were allowed** to take pictures of the aircraft. (passive sentence)*

Note: We don't use the passive voice in the present perfect continuous, the past perfect continuous, the future continuous or the future perfect continuous.

Tense	Active voice	Passive voice
Present simple	She **makes** a phone call.	A phone call **is made**.
Present continuous	She **is making** a phone call.	A phone call **is being made**.
Present perfect simple	She **has made** a phone call.	A phone call **has been made**.
Past simple	She **made** a phone call.	A phone call **was made**.
Past continuous	She **was making** a phone call.	A phone call **was being made**.
Past perfect simple	She **had made** a phone call.	A phone call **had been made**.
Future simple	She **will make** a phone call.	A phone call **will be made**.
Future perfect simple	She **will have made** a phone call.	A phone call **will have been made**.
be going to	She **is going to make** a phone call.	A phone call **is going to be made**.

2 Complete the sentences with the present simple passive, the present continuous passive or the present perfect simple passive. Use the words in brackets.

1 When there is an emergency, a lifeguard _____*is called*_____ . (call)

2 Unfortunately, people _____ when an earthquake strikes. (often injure)

3 Mr Steven _____ , so we can't start the meeting. (delay)

4 My car _____ at the moment. (not service)

5 Our new furniture _____ yet. (not delivered)

6 Security checks _____ at the airport. (frequently carry out)

7 Houses in the countryside _____ . (often not break into)

8 The school children _____ from the building right now. (rescue)

3 Complete the text with the past simple passive, the past continuous passive or the past perfect simple passive. Use the verbs in brackets.

The volcanic eruptions in Iceland

Although the Eyjafjallajökull volcanic eruption in spring 2010 was quite small, severe problems (1) _____*were caused*_____ (cause) in Iceland and all around Europe. In the areas near the eruption, farmers and their families (2) _____ (evacuate), and flights to and from Iceland (3) _____ (postpone). Seismic activity in the area (4) _____ (detect) towards the end of 2009 before a small eruption occurred in mid March 2010. While this eruption wasn't particularly large, in April 2010 an ash cloud (5) _____ (create). This time, it wasn't just flights to and from Iceland that (6) _____ (affect). In actual fact, flights all around Europe (7) _____ (cancel) for a number of days. By mid May the situation had improved, and the volcano (8) _____ (consider) dormant once again.

4 Rewrite the sentences with the future simple passive, the passive of *be going to* or the future perfect simple passive.

1 The painter will paint my uncle's house next week.
  My uncle's house will be painted (by the painter) next week.

2 The gardener is going to plant some new flowers.
  _____

3 The dentist will have taken out your tooth by tomorrow.
  _____

4 They aren't going to exhibit the Monet paintings in Rome.
  _____

5 Will the chef have cooked all the food by tonight?
  _____

6 The cleaners won't have cleaned the building by tomorrow morning.
  _____

7 Will he publish his new book this year?
  _____

8 They won't deliver Mum's new car tomorrow.
  _____

5 Look at the pictures and complete the sentences. Use the correct form of the passive and these verbs.

cut down   extinguish   ~~find~~   hit   need   present

1 Hopefully, the shipwreck in the Caribbean Sea
____will be found____ soon.

2 The fire _____ at
the moment.

International Coastal Cleanup
KEEP OUR BEACHES CLEAN
Volunteers needed

3 Volunteers _____ to help
clean up the beaches.

4 Every day, far too many trees
_____ in the rainforests.

5 While I was paying for my shopping, my car
_____ by another car.

6 Last night, the lifeguard _____
with an award for his bravery.

6 Complete the questions with the correct form of the passive voice using the words in brackets. Then complete the short answers.

1 ____Was that film made____ in New York last year? (that film / make)
Yes, ____it was____ .

2 _____ every afternoon? (tea / serve)
No, _____ .

3 _____ when I visited last night? (twins / feed)
Yes, _____ .

4 _____ at the moment? (the restaurant / renovate)
No, _____ .

5 _____ in the school magazine last week? (my article / publish)
Yes, _____ .

6 _____ tomorrow evening? (the TV / deliver)
No, _____ .

7 _____ a grant? (you / ever give)
Yes, _____ .

8 _____ by the time the guests arrive? (all the food / cook)
Yes, _____ .

7 Complete the second sentences so that they have a similar meaning to the first sentences. Use the words in bold.

1 The government's decision has affected everyone. **been**

Everyone _____ has been affected _____ by the government's decision.

2 Many people use the tram every day. **used**

The tram _____ every day.

3 Thousands of spectators watched the World Cup final. **by**

The World Cup final _____ thousands of spectators.

4 The TV channel broadcast the Eurovision Song Contest last night. **was**

The Eurovision Song Contest _____ last night.

5 The local council will open the castle soon. **be**

The castle _____ by the local council soon.

6 They are going to give my favourite actor a role in the new blockbuster film. **going**

My favourite actor _____ a role in the new blockbuster film.

7 At the zoo, the teacher let the children pet the animals. **allowed**

At the zoo, the children _____ the animals.

8 I have a lot of work to do before I can go out. **must**

My work _____ I can go out.

8 Complete the article with the correct form of the active or passive voice. Use the verbs in brackets.

Médecins Sans Frontières

Médecins Sans Frontières is an organisation that (1) _____ is known _____ (know) for the medical assistance it (2) _____ (offer) to victims of natural or man-made disasters, or to people living in countries that (3) _____ (involve) in war.

Médecins Sans Frontières (4) _____ (establish) in 1971 by a few French doctors, who (5) _____ (believe) that everyone should be able to receive medical care. For about 40 years now, health care and medical training (6) _____ (give) to people in many different countries thanks to this organisation.

The organisation (7) _____ (refer) to as Médecins Sans Frontières worldwide, but English-speaking countries often use the name 'Doctors Without Borders'. There are five operational centres, which (8) _____ (locate) in Amsterdam, Barcelona, Brussels, Geneva and Paris. Since the creation of Médecins Sans Frontières, private contributors (9) _____ (provide) most of the organisation's funding. The organisation (10) _____ (present) with the Nobel Peace Prize in 1999 for the work it does.

9 Say it! Imagine that you are arranging for help to be sent to a country which has been hit by an earthquake. Talk with your partner about what has been done and what will be done. Use the passive voice and these ideas to help you.

- food / deliver
- clothes / gather
- money / collect
- medical personnel / fly out
- medicines / send
- inhabitants / evacuate
- homes / provide
- rescue workers / call
- fresh water / distribute

Lots of food has been delivered to the people.

Medical personnel will be flown out.

1 **Read.**

I like playing in matches. I really wanted to be picked by the coach.

Passive voice: gerunds, infinitives and modals

The **passive voice** can be used with **gerunds, infinitives** and with **modal** verbs.

	Active voice	**Passive voice**
infinitive	She needs **to make** a phone call.	A phone call needs **to be made**.
gerund	She likes people **calling** her.	She likes **being called**.
modals (present)	She **may make** a phone call.	A phone call **may be made**.
modals (past)	She **may have made** a phone call.	A phone call **may have been made**.

Note: When the verb **make** means **force**, it is followed by the bare infinitive in the active voice, but in the passive voice it is followed by the full infinitive.
I **make** my daughter **set** the alarm every morning.
My daughter **is made** to set the alarm every morning.

However, when verbs of perception such as **hear** and **see** are used in passive sentences, they can be followed by a gerund or the full infinitive.
I **heard** the children **playing** with the ball.
The children **were heard playing** with the ball.
I **saw** the man **take** the money.
The man **was seen to take** the money.

2 **Circle the correct words.**

1 The ironing needs **to be done** / do.

2 The letter shouldn't **be opened / open**.

3 We were made **to stay / stay** behind.

4 All the children wanted **to be chosen / choosing**.

5 The boy was seen **break / breaking** the window.

6 An exception **may have been made / may be made** now.

3 Choose the correct answers.

1 An aircraft _____ above the island.
   a seen to fly
   b was seen flying *(circled)*
   c be flying

2 Living conditions in the area should _____ .
   a be improved
   b being improved
   c to be improved

3 The man _____ dishonest.
   a was known to be
   b knows
   c was known to being

4 Overalls ought to _____ by all factory employees from now on.
   a wear
   b be worn
   c have been worn

5 Luke dislikes _____ by his surname.
   a be called
   b to be called
   c being called

6 A state of emergency must _____ immediately.
   a be declared
   b being declared
   c declared

7 You were very lucky. You could _____ very badly.
   a be hurt
   b being hurt
   c have been hurt

8 Nobody wants _____ .
   a to be taken advantage of
   b being taken advantage of
   c to have taken advantage of

4 Complete the sentences in the passive voice. Use the words in bold.

1 Jamila hopes they choose her to speak at the debate. **be**
   Jamila hopes _____to be chosen_____ to speak at the debate.

2 I can't believe the traffic warden gave me a fine. **given**
   I was surprised _____ a fine by the traffic warden.

3 The lifeguard saw the little girl crying for help. **was**
   The little girl _____ for help by the lifeguard.

4 The firefighters made us leave the forest. **to**
   We _____ the forest by the firefighters.

5 Tod wishes they hadn't chosen him for the main role in the play. **for**
   Tod regrets _____ the main role in the play.

6 I won't let them punish me for something I didn't do. **punished**
   I refuse _____ for something I didn't do.

7 Our teacher doesn't let us use calculators during the maths lesson. **allowed**
   We _____ calculators during the maths lesson.

8 Children love it when their parents take them to the park. **being**
   Children love _____ the park by their parents.

5 Complete the sentences with the passive voice. Use these verbs.

clean   hire   ignore   ~~pay~~   photograph   repair   take   win

1 Your mortgage must _____be paid_____ soon.

2 Jonathon hates _____ by people.

3 Our dining room table needs _____ by a carpenter.

4 Wimbledon should _____ by Andy Murray next year.

5 We were made _____ up the mess.

6 The chef considered _____ on a part time basis.

7 All the actors wanted _____ on the red carpet.

8 Most children enjoy _____ to the zoo.

6 Write sentences using the passive voice.

1 Tom / dislike / tell off
   Tom dislikes being told off.

2 the animals / must / feed / twice a day
   _____

3 ? / Jessica / look forward / make / a supervisor
   _____

4 my sister and I / like / invite / to parties
   _____

5 ? / you / appreciate / tell / the truth
   _____

6 a new sports centre / may / build / next summer
   _____

7 I / make / tidy / my bedroom / every Saturday
   _____

8 they / not want / left behind / last night
   _____

7 Say it! Imagine that your head teacher wants to make some changes at school and has asked for your suggestions. Talk with your partner about what you would suggest, using the passive voice and these ideas to help you.

- bigger playground / create
- science lab / build
- whiteboards / install
- other languages / introduce
- school / renovate
- food / improve
- sports facilities / construct
- more teachers / hire

In my opinion, a bigger playground should be created.

I think a science lab must be built.

1 Read.

Even though, although, despite, in spite of, however and whereas

The following **linking words** and phrases can be used to introduce an idea that is the opposite of or contrasts with another idea.

Even though and **although** are followed by a subject and verb.
Even though/Although we played surprisingly well, we lost the match.

Despite and **in spite of** are followed by a noun, a pronoun or a gerund.
Despite/In spite of the risk, Joe jumped into the sea to save the little girl.
Despite/In spite of his wealth, he was very mean.
Despite/In spite of being off duty, the nurse helped us.

Note: We can use **the fact (that)** + subject and verb after **despite** and **in spite of**.
Despite/In spite of the fact (that) there was an emergency exit, it was blocked!

When **even though, although, despite** and **in spite of** come at the beginning of the sentence, we use a comma to separate the two clauses. But when they come in the middle of a sentence between two clauses to show the contrast between them, we don't use a comma.
Despite doing my best, I didn't manage to finish on time.
I didn't manage to finish on time despite doing my best.

However and **whereas** are also used to add a comment which contrasts with what has just been said.
However is followed by a comma, but we put a comma before **whereas**.
*Kim is a great nurse. **However,** she can't stand the sight of blood!*
*I like to go out, **whereas** my sister prefers to stay home.*

2 **Circle the correct words.**

1   **Whereas / (Even though)** they are rivals on the football pitch, they are best friends at school.

2   **However / Even though** there are more police officers controlling the traffic, congestion is on the increase.

3   The criminal was convicted. **Whereas / However**, he wasn't sent to prison.

4   Jenny said that nobody was hurt in the accident, **whereas / despite** I heard that three people were sent to hospital.

5   **In spite of / Although** the road being blocked, Tara got to her interview on time.

6   We got to the station early. **However / Although**, we still managed to miss the train.

7   **Although / However** many people came to the party, a lot of food was left over.

8   We went to the beach **even though / in spite of the fact** that the weather was bad.

9   **Despite / Although** the problems, Paul was successful.

10   Tina wants to be a police officer when she grows up, **in spite of / whereas** Jake wants to be a firefighter.

3 **Match.**

1   Despite the hurricane,

2   There was a hit and run incident in the town centre.

3   I still speak to Jack

4   Although the earthquake didn't last for long,

5   In spite of caring about the environment,

6   Jodie is constantly on a diet

7   Despite the problems they have,

8   My sister loves chocolate ice cream,

a   despite the fact that she is slim.

b   even though he lied to me.

c   they are very optimistic about the future.

d   However, nobody was seriously injured.

e   the death toll was surprisingly high.

f   the inhabitants weren't evacuated.

g   whereas I love vanilla.

h   George never recycles anything.

4 **Complete the text with these words.**

~~although~~   despite   even though   however   in spite   whereas

(1) _____Although_____ everyone knows about the police, ambulance and fire services, there are other emergency services that are less well known. In Britain, one of the most important services is the one provided by the Royal National Lifeboat Service (RNLI). (2) _____ the British Isles have a long history of seafaring, the rescue service for people in trouble at sea is not provided by the government. All of the lifeboat men and women are volunteers, (3) _____ most ambulance workers and firefighters are employed full-time to do that job. (4) _____ this, the RNLI rescue teams are highly trained experts who find time to help others (5) _____ of their other commitments. Because of their generosity, sailors know that they can call for help when they get into trouble. (6) _____ , no one should go to sea without proper training. To do this would put your life and the lives of the rescuers at risk.

5 Combine the sentences using the words in bold.

1 Freddy jumped over the fence. He didn't hurt himself. **in spite of**

   In spite of jumping over the fence, Freddy didn't hurt himself.

2 Maria is a great tennis player. She wasn't voted player of the year at her tennis club. **even though**

   _____

3 Danielle is a great volleyball player. She wasn't chosen for the team. **being**

   _____

4 Thousands of fans turned up to the cup final. There wasn't any trouble. **even though**

   _____

5 Rosie lives in a beautiful neighbourhood. There's litter everywhere. **although**

   _____

6 Vandals broke into my car last night. It was parked opposite a police station. **despite the fact that**

   _____

7 John accused me of stealing his calculator. I believe he lost it. **whereas**

   _____

8 My parents are quite open-minded. They don't want me to become an actor. **although**

   _____

6 Say it! Look at the newspaper headlines and talk with your partner about the situations using linking words.

Floods hit region – no casualties!

Economic crisis – thousands of smartphones bought every day!!

Trouble expected in central London – protest went well!

Bomb scare – Metro not closed!

Thieves caught red-handed — weren't prosecuted!

More accidents in town centre – no plans for traffic control

Man suspected of arson – no evidence!

Despite the floods, there were no casualties in the region.

ADVERSE WEATHER CONDITIONS – MATCH TO GO AHEAD!

Even though the police expected trouble in central London, the protest went surprisingly well.

1 **Complete the sentences with direct or reported speech.**

1 'I'm starting my French course tomorrow,' Kelly said.

   Kelly said ____(that) she was starting her French course the following/next day____ .

2 The maths teacher told Billy to stop talking.

   _____ the maths teacher told Billy.

3 'There was a bad accident in the centre of London last week,' Dad said.

   Dad said _____ .

4 'Please can you water the plants for me tonight?' Aunt Poppy asked me.

   Aunt Poppy asked me _____ .

5 'Where is the sports complex?' my brother asked.

   My brother asked _____ .

6 'Were you revising all night?' Tony asked his sister.

   Tony asked his sister _____ .

7 'You will get a good mark for your essay,' the university lecturer told me.

   The university lecturer told me _____ .

8 'Could you post a letter for me, please?' my boss asked.

   My boss asked _____ .

9 Mum told me not to go out in the storm that night.

   _____ Mum told me.

10 'The employees must have a lunch break,' the manager said.

   The manager said _____ .

11 'We watched a film before dinner,' the children said.

   The children said _____ .

12 'Did you lie to your brother?' Dad asked me.

   Dad asked me _____ .

2 **Choose the correct answers.**

1 Jeremy offered _____ to the station.
   a driving me
   (b) to drive me
   c drive me

2 The doctor advised _____ less meat.
   a Mum to eat
   b Mum eats
   c that Mum ate

3 My best friend announced _____ the competition.
   a has won
   b she wins
   c that she had won

4 Harry apologised for _____ my favourite game.
   a damaging
   b he damaged
   c has damaged

5 Natasha promised _____ her grandparents.
   a visiting
   b to visit
   c visit

6 My dad reminded _____ my keys.
   a taking
   b to take
   c me to take

3 **Circle the correct words.**

On Tuesday, 12th January 2010, Haiti (1) **struck /** (**was struck**) by a huge earthquake that registered a magnitude of 7.0. It was a disaster and hundreds of thousands of people (2) **lost / were lost** their lives. The rescuers calculated that nearly one-third of the country's entire population (3) **were being affected / had been affected** by the quake.

The Haitian Government estimated that 250,000 homes and 30,000 commercial buildings had collapsed or (4) **damaged / had been severely damaged**. This meant that communication systems (5) **broke down / were broken down**, many roads (6) **blocked / were blocked** and many hospitals (7) **were destroyed / destroyed**, which made the situation even worse.

The world didn't hesitate to act. Aid (8) **received / was received** from many different countries, a variety of fund raising activities (9) **set up / were set up** worldwide, and money and goods (10) **are donated / were donated** by countless individuals.

4 **Write sentences in the passive voice.**

1 Judy loves her dad driving her to school.

 Judy loves being driven to school by her dad.

2 All candidates must fill in this information.

 _____

3 They won't renovate the town hall this summer.

 _____

4 The bricklayer was mixing the cement at seven o'clock this morning.

 _____

5 I've already walked the dogs.

 _____

6 France produces a lot of different types of cheese.

 _____

5 **Complete the article with these words.**

although despite however ~~in spite~~ though whereas

Chocolate tasting – a delicious job?

Did you know that some people taste chocolate for a living? (1) ____In spite____ of sounding like the best job in the world, chocolate tasting is not always easy.

What do chocolate tasters do? To begin with, they do a lot of market research and hold tasting sessions to determine what appeals to consumers. (2) _____ the research, the taster still needs to actually try samples of chocolate. Even (3) _____ there is no set time when chocolates are sampled, most of the tasting is done early in the morning. The tester needs to be slightly hungry and to be far away from anything else with strong tastes or smells.

You may think that tasters sample lots of chocolates in one day. (4) _____, they can only test up to six different chocolates at a time. Successful chocolate tasters can understand what 'good' chocolate is.

(5) _____ they train themselves to predict which chocolates will be successful, they sometimes make mistakes, and as a result, some of the chocolates chosen aren't a hit with consumers.

Most people believe the chocolate tasters are only interested in the taste of the chocolate, (6) _____ they also pay attention to the way it looks, feels and smells during the tasting session.

WRITING PROJECT

6 **Look at a project about a mountain rescue service. Choose the correct answers.**

Mountain rescue

Mountain rescue is a tremendously important service. Its goal is to enable the safe return of people who (1) _____ or have got lost while exploring a mountainous environment. Rescue is usually very difficult and can even be dangerous for the rescue team. Helicopters (2) _____ to rescue people, and search dogs may be used to locate injured or lost people.

This photo shows a rescue helicopter in the Denali National Park, where many rescues (3) _____ . The national park (4) _____ in Alaska, and it boasts Denali, the highest mountain in North America. Many visitors flock to the national park, which (5) _____ in 1917, for mountain expeditions. (6) _____ climbers are well aware of the dangers they face, many accidents occur as some climbers aren't prepared for the adverse weather conditions they will encounter. (7) _____ of being warned before they set off, they (8) _____ to depend on rescue services for a safe return.

1	**a** injured	**b** have been injured	**c** are injuring
2	**a** are often used	**b** often used	**c** used
3	**a** are carried out	**b** carry out	**c** carried out
4	**a** locates	**b** are located	**c** is located
5	**a** established	**b** is established	**c** was established
6	**a** Although	**b** Despite	**c** In spite of
7	**a** In spite	**b** Even though	**c** Despite
8	**a** are forced often	**b** are often forced	**c** are often being forced

7 **Now it's your turn to do a project about a rescue service. Find or draw a picture of the rescue service and write about it.**

1 Read.

I love your gorgeous new hat.

Oh, thanks. The more I wear it, the more I like it.

Adjectives

When we use two or more adjectives to describe a noun, we usually place the adjectives in the following order:

opinion	size	age	shape	colour	origin	material	noun
beautiful				green		silk	scarf
expensive		new			Italian		suit
	huge		ancient			marble	statue

We can use adjectives after verbs like **appear, be, become, feel, get, look, make, seem, smell, sound, taste** and **turn**. Sometimes we put an adverb between the verb and the adjective.
*That dress **looks amazing** on you!*
*I **feel very hot** in this sweater.*

2 Put the words in the correct order to make sentences.

1 silk / bought / expensive / Rebecca / an / scarf / red

   <u>Rebecca bought an expensive red silk scarf.</u>

2 white / the / was / girl / a / straw / wearing / huge / hat

   _____

3 black / prefers / linen / model / the / stylish / dress / the

   _____

4 beautiful / rug / a / old / my parents / have got

   _____

5 round / don't like / table / huge / wooden / that / I

   _____

6 little / drives / amazing / French / Grandpa / an / car

   _____

Comparison of adjectives

We use the comparative form of adjectives to compare two people, animals or things. We often use the word **than** after the comparative.
*Heidi is **older than** her brother.*
*Your skirt is **longer than** mine.*

We use the **superlative** form of adjectives to compare a person, animal or thing with other people, animals or things.
We use the word **the** before the **superlative**.
*This is **the most expensive** pair of shoes I've ever bought!*
*She's **the most stylish** of all the mothers.*

These adjectives have irregular comparative and superlative forms:

Adjective	Comparative	Superlative
good	better	the best
bad	worse	the worst
much	more	the most
many	more	the most
little	less	the least
far	further / farther	the furthest / farthest

3 **Complete the sentences with the comparative or superlative. Use the adjectives in brackets.**

1 This is <u>the most wonderful</u> festival in the country. (wonderful)

2 Catherine's cowboy boots were _____ mine. (expensive)

3 The new boutique in the town centre sells _____ clothes on the market. (trendy)

4 Max is _____ student in my class. (good)

5 Penny is much _____ her sister. (glamorous)

6 Your ball gown is _____ Susie's. (long)

7 Henrietta is wearing _____ diamond I've ever seen! (big)

8 Today's weather forecast is _____ yesterday's. (bad)

(not) as … as

We can also use **as + adjective + as** to compare two people, animals or things.
We use **as … as** when the two people, animals or things are the same.
*Rebecca is **as** talented **as** her father.*

We use **not as … as** when the two people, animals or things are not the same.
*This costume isn't **as** impressive **as** the first one.*

4 **Complete the sentences so they have a similar meaning to the first sentences. Use *as … as* and *not as … as*.**

1 The weather is very nice today. The weather wasn't so nice yesterday.
The weather yesterday <u>wasn't as nice as</u> it is today.

2 My dad's watch is expensive. My mum's watch is also expensive.
My dad's watch _____ my mum's watch.

3 I like burgers, but they aren't very healthy. Salads are very healthy.
Burgers _____ salads.

4 Mrs Hilton is a fashionable woman. Her daughter is also fashionable.
Mrs Hilton _____ her daughter.

5 Steve can run very far because he is really fit. Jemima can only run a hundred metres.
Jemina _____ Steve.

6 I washed my bike today. My brother hasn't washed his bike for a month.
My brother's bike _____ my bike.

the + comparative ..., the + comparative ...

We can use **the** + comparative ..., **the** + comparative ... to show that something depends on or is influenced by something else. It shows cause and effect.
***The older** he gets, **the more handsome** he becomes.*
***The more** Judy goes out, **the happier** she feels.*

5 Look at these situations and write sentences using *the* + comparative ..., *the* + comparative ... .

1 Emily is training very hard. She is becoming better at playing tennis.

   <u>The harder Emily trains, the better she becomes at playing tennis.</u>

2 I've been eating more fruit and vegetables. I've started to feel better.

   _____

3 Our teacher is giving us more homework. We are complaining more.

   _____

4 Jerry works a lot of overtime. He's feeling tired.

   _____

5 We are going to more concerts these days. We are spending more money.

   _____

6 I like easy puzzles. They are very enjoyable.

   _____

7 John and James have been studying very hard. Their marks are getting better.

   _____

8 You aren't being very friendly these days. Your friend is getting upset.

   _____

6 Choose the correct answers.

1 The more healthily you eat, the _____ to lose weight.
   a more likely you are ⟵(circled)
   b you are more likely
   c you are the most likely

2 My new skirt is _____ as Martha's vintage one.
   a more original
   b not as original
   c the most original

3 This is _____ maths exercise I've ever done!
   a more complicated than
   b more complicated
   c the most complicated

4 Celia has been looking for a(n) _____ necklace.
   a unusual pearl white
   b white pearl unusual
   c unusual white pearl

5 _____ people buy designer clothes nowadays than in the past.
   a The fewer
   b Fewer
   c The fewest

6 Frankie isn't _____ as you think.
   a the most old-fashioned
   b as old-fashioned
   c more old-fashioned

7 Jodie's parents gave her a _____ kitten.
   a gorgeous black tiny
   b gorgeous tiny black
   c black gorgeous tiny

8 I think watching films online _____ as going to the cinema.
   a is enjoyable as
   b is more enjoyable
   c is as enjoyable

7 **Circle the correct words.**

Elitist clothing, which is one of (1) **more popular / ~~the most popular~~** brands amongst teenagers today, was founded in 1973. It offers a wide variety of clothing and sportswear, and although the items may be slightly (2) **more expensive / the most expensive** than other brands of clothing, they are (3) **the most fashionable / as fashionable as** on the market and are becoming even (4) **as popular as / more popular** with young people. These clothes may (5) **not be as economical as / be the most economical** non-brand clothes, but they are very unique. However, the more people wear these brands, (6) **the less unique / the more unique** they become.

The company also sells Wave clothing, items which are just (7) **as trendy as / the trendiest** Elitist and are very popular with skateboard enthusiasts. So, if you're keen on (8) **cool long multicoloured / multicoloured long cool** swimming trunks, try Elitist!

8 **Complete the second sentences so they have a similar meaning to the first sentences. Use the words in bold.**

1 Veronica is the rudest person I've ever met. **as**

I've never met anybody _____*as rude as*_____ Veronica.

2 When it gets hot, it's easy for me to dive into the pool. **easier**

The hotter it gets, _____ for me to dive into the pool.

3 Henrietta's clothes are more old-fashioned than her sister's. **trendy**

Henrietta's clothes _____ her sister's.

4 I've never seen such an amazing coat. **most**

This is _____ I've ever seen.

5 Felicity is more successful than Natasha. **not**

Natasha is _____ Felicity.

6 Expensive clothing is usually of better quality. **better**

Usually, the more expensive clothing is, _____ it is.

7 It takes one hour to fly to Amman. It takes five hours to drive there. **is**

Flying to Amman _____ driving there.

8 I think running is tiring. I think swimming is tiring, too. **as**

I think running _____ swimming.

9 **Say it! Look at these pictures with your partner. Describe and compare these mobile phones. Use these suggestions to help you.**

- small / big
- cheap / expensive
- modern / old-fashioned
- simple / sophisticated

Number 3 is a beautiful modern mobile phone.

Number 1 must be more expensive than number 2.

1 **Read.**

Adverbs (manner, place, time, degree)

Adverbs of manner (**slowly, fast, beautifully, easily, quickly, nicely**, etc.) tell us how something happens. They answer the question **How ...?** They are often formed by adding **–ly** to adjectives.
*Our drama teacher sings **beautifully**.*

Adverbs of place (**here, there, inside, outside, beside, opposite, in the cinema,** etc.) tell us where something happens. They answer the question **Where ...?**
***Where** is the boutique?*
*The boutique is **over there**.*

Adverbs of time (**yesterday, today, tomorrow, later, last year, now**, etc.) tell us when something happens. They answer the question **When ...?**
***When** are you going to the fashion show?*
*We are going to the fashion show **tomorrow evening**.*

Adverbs of degree (**enough, quite, rather, too, so, very, extremely, absolutely**, etc.) tell us **how much** or **how many** there is of something or the extent of something.
- adverb + **enough** + full infinitive
  *She can't sing **well enough** to become a singer.*
- **quite** + adverb
  *Alex runs **quite fast**.*
- **rather** + adverb
  *It's **rather late**.*
- **too** + adverb + full infinitive
  *We arrived at the play **too late to see** the opening act.*
- **so** + adverb
  *I didn't realise you spoke Italian **so well**.*
- **very/really** + adverb
  *You dance **really gracefully!***
- **extremely** + adverb
  *You did **extremely well** in the exams.*

Note: When we have two or more adverbs in a sentence, they usually come in the following order:
VERB + manner, place, time
*Mum **looked quickly around the shop this morning**.*

However, when there are verbs in the sentence that show movement, (**come, go, leave, arrive,** etc.) the order is:
VERB + place, manner, time
*Sarah **arrived at the theatre by car at half past six**.*

Some **adverbs of manner** can go before or after the main verb, or at the end of a sentence.
*John **quickly** walked out of the room.*
*John walked **quickly** out of the room.*
*John walked out of the room **quickly**.*

2 **Identify the type of adverb in bold.**

1 He's walking **so** slowly because he's hurt his foot.   degree

2 I'm so happy because my grandparents arrived **yesterday**.   _____

3 The book I've just read was **quite** boring.   _____

4 Whenever we have a maths test, Jason does really **well**.   _____

5 It's **too** late to go to the supermarket now.   _____

6 Lynda runs extremely **fast**. I'm sure she'll win the race.   _____

7 You told me to put the bags over **there**.   _____

8 I love sitting **outside** when it's a nice day.   _____

3 **Look at the pictures and complete the sentences. Use these words.**

> here   in   inside   opposite   outside   there

1 Robbie left his guitar
   ___here___ and now it's gone!

2 Due to heavy rain, the concert
   will take place _____ .

3 There's the chemist's. It's on the
   _____ side of the road.

4 Josh is waiting _____
   the fish and chip shop.

5 Why are you sitting over
   _____ on your own?

6 Joanne opened the door and
   walked _____ .

4 **Rewrite the sentences, putting the adverbs in brackets in the correct place. Sometimes more than one answer is possible.**

1 Marcus waited outside the head teacher's office. (nervously)
   Marcus (nervously) waited (nervously) outside the head teacher's office (nervously).

2 The gold medallist's father stood beside his son. (proudly)
   _____

3 Jodie crossed the road. (hurriedly)
   _____

4 The band members walked out of the audition. (quietly)
   _____

5 When the bell rang, the school children ran outside to play. (happily)
   _____

6 Dad agreed to sing at the wedding reception tomorrow evening. (willingly)
   _____

7 The school girl gave up her seat on the bus. (reluctantly)
   _____

8 My cousin looked at my new silver earrings. (enviously)
   _____

5 Write the words in the correct order to make sentences.

1 absolutely / I'm / by / fascinated / folk music
   <u>I'm absolutely fascinated by folk music.</u>

2 has always / violin / she / extremely / played / the / well
   _____

3 Salma / to school / rather / walked / quickly
   _____

4 so / speaks / Marcus / Spanish / well
   _____

5 too / you / dangerously / live
   _____

6 happily / in the park / the children / this morning / ran
   _____

7 fast / doesn't drive / Samantha / enough
   _____

8 the question / read / please / carefully
   _____

9 to go / too / it's / early / to bed
   _____

10 waited / impatiently / yesterday afternoon / I / in front of the school gates
   _____

Comparison of adverbs

When an adverb has the same form as the adjective, we usually add **–er** to make the comparative and **–est** to make the superlative.

early	earlier	the earliest
fast	faster	the fastest
hard	harder	the hardest
high	higher	the highest
late	later	the latest

When an adverb ends in **–ly**, we use **more/less** to make the comparative form and **the most/the least** to make the superlative form.

beautifully	more/less beautifully	the most/the least beautifully
loudly	more/less loudly	the most/the least loudly

Some adverbs have irregular comparative and superlative forms.

badly	worse	the worst
far	farther/further	the farthest/the furthest
little	less	the least
much	more	the most
well	better	the best

6 Complete the sentences with the comparative or superlative form. Use the adverbs in brackets.

1 Sandra takes her singing lessons <u>less/more seriously than</u> Elisa. (seriously)

2 Henry works _____ of all the employees. (fast)

3 Isabel behaved _____ I had expected. (badly)

4 My cousins live _____ away from the city than we do. (far)

5 Who got _____ exam results in the class? (well)

6 You all danced well; however, Julie danced _____ . (gracefully)

7 Mrs Harris always explains things _____ Mr Daniels. (clearly)

8 The three sisters speak German well, but Olivia speaks it _____ of all. (fluently)

7 **Circle the correct words.**

1 The musicians **noisily were busking / were busking noisily** in the street.

2 The technician **angrily agreed / agreed angry** to do a sound check.

3 Frank trained **much hardly / harder than** we had anticipated for the tennis final.

4 I'm **so / too** glad you are able to join us!

5 Dad finds jazz music **extremely / enough** inspiring.

6 We **genuinely forgot / forgot genuinely** about the dress rehearsal.

7 Carly eats **the least healthily / less healthily than** her brother.

8 I believe our chemistry teacher communicates with us the **most effectively / more effectively**.

8 **The words in bold are wrong. Write the correct words.**

1 Brian is really talented and draws **beautiful**.   *beautifully*

2 I studied hard for the exams and I did very **good**.   _____

3 Josh doesn't run as **faster** as Peter.   _____

4 Please give me a lift because it's raining **inside**.   _____

5 We won't go to the beach today as it's **cold quite**.   _____

6 Ben and Mike tidied their bedroom **quicker** this morning.   _____

7 Don't **loudly speak** in the library.   _____

8 I'm **to** tired to go out tonight.   _____

9 I don't want any more pizza. I've had **absolutely** to eat.   _____

10 My sister solves crossword puzzles **the most** easily than me.   _____

9 **Say it! Imagine you are a children's TV programme presenter. Talk with your partner about what instructions you would give them to make jelly with fruit and other simple recipes. Use adverbs and these suggestions to help you.**

- cut fruit
- boil water
- put powder in bowl
- add boiled water
- stir until powder has melted
- pour into small bowls
- put in fridge
- take jelly out of the fridge

- carefully
- slowly
- completely
- then
- later
- for five hours

You have to cut the fruit carefully.

Then boil the water.

1 Read.

Adjectives ending in –ing/–ed

Some adjectives can be formed using the present participle ending **–ing** and the past participle ending **–ed**. The **–ing** form is active and describes the effect someone or something has on others. The **–ed** form is passive and describes how someone or something is affected by something or how they feel about it.

*I'm **interested** in sports.*
*Sports are **interesting**.*

*The seminar was **motivating**.*
*I felt **motivated** during the seminar.*

2 Complete the sentences with the adjectives in brackets.

1 I don't know why you're _____ bored _____ during the history of fashion lesson. I don't think it's _____ at all. (boring, bored)

2 The fashion designer's latest show was quite _____ . I'm _____ you haven't heard about his new designs. (surprising, surprised)

3 Helen is _____ in everything to do with the fashion industry and she thinks being a designer must be an _____ job. (interesting, interested)

4 I was really _____ when I heard the fire alarm ringing. It was one of the most _____ experiences I've ever had. (frightening, frightened)

5 John's teacher was _____ by his designs. He actually said, 'They are simply _____!' (amazing, amazed)

6 The film we saw last night was _____ . I was so _____ that I closed my eyes. (terrifying, terrified)

3 Circle the correct words.

1 I find classical music extremely **bored / boring**.

2 Joe was **flattered / flattering** when the band members asked him to sing with them.

3 Visiting Stonehenge was a **fascinated / fascinating** experience for me.

4 Elizabeth's job is very **fulfilled / fulfilling**.

5 Margo's account of why she arrived late wasn't very **convinced / convincing**.

6 When I do yoga, I feel extremely **relaxed / relaxing**.

7 Falling down the cliff was a **horrified / horrifying** experience.

8 Aren't you **disappointed / disappointing** that your best friend couldn't come to the match?

4 Complete the sentences with the correct form of adjectives formed from the words in brackets.

1 Taking part in the concert was the most _____ amazing _____ experience ever! (amaze)

2 We were _____ to hear that Susie wanted to give up singing lessons. (surprise)

3 Harry has been feeling very _____ lately. (depress)

4 The conductor looked very _____ . (confuse)

5 The students weren't _____ in learning about the Stone Age. (interest)

6 I've been practising all day and now I'm _____ . (exhaust)

7 Mainstream fashion is so _____ . (bore)

8 The story of the orphan's childhood was very _____ . (move)

5 Complete the sentences with the correct form of adjectives formed from these verbs.

| alarm amuse annoy confuse depress stimulate tire worry |

1 It's _____ alarming _____ how thin those children are.

2 My brother hasn't been eating lately and I'm _____ about him.

3 Training on a daily basis is very _____ .

4 Marcus is bored. He needs a more _____ job.

5 Stop repeating whatever I say! It's so _____ .

6 Ian has lost his new tablet and he feels really _____ .

7 I really don't understand. I'm truly _____ .

8 Stop laughing. It really isn't at all _____ .

Adjectives and infinitives

Adjectives can often be followed by the full infinitive. Sometimes there is an object or a noun after the adjective.

*Lizzy is always **happy to lend** Sally her denim jacket.*
*Making your own evening dress is a **great way to save money**!*

6 Write the words in the correct order to make sentences.

1 my homework / willing / me / is / with / to / Khaled / help
<u>Khaled is willing to help me with my homework.</u>

2 to / a / idea / wear / clothes / it's / a job interview / smart / to / good
_____

3 glad / is / my / progress / maths / to / my / teacher / see
_____

4 a / way / Pilates / release / fantastic / stress / is / to
_____

5 to / was / her promotion / Dina / announce / proud
_____

6 activity / is / tiring / gardening / a / very
_____

7 the / to / delighted / hear / I / news / was / good
_____

8 film / is / great / watch / *Frozen* / to / a
_____

7 Say it! Talk with your partner and exchange opinions about these things. Practise using some of the adjectives you have learnt.

- shopping
- playing computer games
- swimming
- hiking
- watching comedies
- learning a foreign language
- doing your homework

Shopping is boring.

I get bored when I go shopping!

1 Read.

The children cooked the turkey all by themselves.

Reflexive pronouns

We use **reflexive pronouns**
- when the subject and the object of the sentence are the same.
  *I gave **myself** a year to get used to life in the city.*
- with some verbs (**behave, blame, cut, enjoy, help, hurt,** etc.).
  *You shouldn't blame **yourself** for the team's defeat.*
- when we want to say that somebody does something alone or without somebody else's help. We often use the word **by**.
  *We managed to cook dinner by **ourselves**.*

Singular	Plural
myself	ourselves
yourself	yourselves
himself	themselves
herself	
itself	

2 Complete the sentences with reflexive pronouns.

1 Mr Henry introduced _____**himself**_____ to the students.

2 My mum sometimes talks to _____ when she is stressed.

3 Sally, did you make all this food by _____ ?

4 I shouldn't blame _____ for the accident, but I can't help it.

5 My sister and I injured _____ during the hike.

6 We must wash _____ to keep clean.

7 I painted my bedroom all by _____ .

8 Our school band members see _____ as professional musicians.

Indefinite pronouns

An **indefinite pronoun** refers to one or more unspecified beings, things or places.

We use **somebody, someone** and **something** to talk about a person or thing in affirmative sentences.
Someone rang me late last night.

We use **anybody, anyone** and **anything** to talk about a person or thing in negative and interrogative sentences.
*I can't see **anything** without my glasses.*
*Is there **anyone** at home?*

We use **everybody, everyone** and **everything** to talk about all people or things. They are used in the singular form.
***Everybody** is enjoying the party.*

We use **nobody, no one** and **nothing** to talk about no person or thing. They have a negative meaning.
***Nobody** likes my cooking!*

3 **Complete the dialogue. Use these words.**

anyone   ~~anything~~   everybody   everything   nobody   nothing   someone   something

Amanda: Ross, do you know (1) ___anything___ about the Lost City of Atlantis? You're very interested in Greek mythology and the ancient world, so you must know (2) _____ .

Ross: OK, I'll tell you (3) _____ I know. First of all, Atlantis means the 'island of Atlas'. Atlas was a mythological character who supported the world on his shoulders. Plato wrote about Atlantis in about 350 BCE. He claimed that it was a beautiful island and that it was located in front of the Pillars of Hercules, which are at the entrance to the Strait of Gibraltar. Plato went on to say that Atlantis sank in one day and one night.

Amanda: Does (4) _____ know how it sank?

Ross: Well, once again, Plato claimed that when Atlantis unsuccessfully tried to conquer Athens, it disappeared.

Amanda: (5) _____ must know the truth, though.

Ross: In antiquity, (6) _____ discussed its existence, but few people actually believed it was fact and not fiction.

Amanda: I see. Is it true that (7) _____ has ever found the lost city?

Ross: Yes, it is. In fact, there is (8) _____ to prove that it is real. However, the legend of Atlantis continues to inspire writers and film producers.

Possessive pronouns

We use **possessive pronouns** to show that something belongs to someone and to avoid repetition of the noun.
*These gloves are **mine**.*

Possessive pronouns replace the possessive adjective and the noun.
*This is **your pencil**. It's **yours**.*

Note: We don't use **its** as a possessive pronoun.

Singular	Plural
mine	ours
yours	yours
his	theirs
hers	
–	

4 **Complete the sentences with the correct possessive pronouns.**

1   Valery didn't take a hat, so I lent her one of _____ mine _____ .

2   I am going to bring my laptop. Dennis doesn't need to bring _____ .

3   Warren, are all these computer games _____ ?

4   I don't have a red bag. It can't be _____ .

5   Since you forgot your mobile, ask Kelly if you can use _____ .

6   You don't have to take your car. We are going to take _____ .

7   My next-door neighbours don't like dogs. The puppy in their garden can't be _____ .

8   Children, are these projects _____ ?

5 **Choose the correct answers.**

1   They want to redecorate their apartment by _____ .
   a themselves *(circled)*
   b somebody
   c theirs

2   Do you have _____ to donate to charity?
   a anything
   b something
   c everything

3   There are enough drinks for _____ .
   a no one
   b someone
   c everyone

4   Are these dictionaries _____ ?
   a yourself
   b everyone
   c anybody's

5   Hannah cut _____ while she was chopping up tomatoes.
   a ourselves
   b myself
   c herself

6   We normally do the gardening _____ .
   a ourselves
   b themselves
   c itself

7   I burnt _____ while I was taking the soufflé out of the oven.
   a me
   b mine
   c myself

8   The archaeologists said that the finds were _____ .
   a everyone
   b theirs
   c no one

9   I can't see _____ through this magnifying glass!
   a nothing
   b everything
   c anything

10   Mike can't use _____ laptop because it has a virus.
   a anyone
   b his
   c himself

11   _____ had a wonderful time at the party. All the children went home happy.
   a Nobody
   b Somebody
   c Everybody

12   I have my own room now. It's all _____ .
   a ours
   b mine
   c his

6 Complete the second sentences so they have a similar meaning to the first sentences. Use the words in bold.

1 Does this laptop belong to you or is it Helen's? **yours**
   Is _____ this laptop yours _____ or is it Helen's?

2 The bracelet on the dressing table belongs to me. **is**
   The bracelet on the dressing table _____ .

3 I didn't have any help making this necklace. **by**
   I made this necklace _____ .

4 Joanna can't see anything without her glasses. **can**
   Joanna _____ without her glasses.

5 I can't believe that Sami made this model plane. **himself**
   I can't believe that Sami made this _____ .

6 There isn't anything on the menu that I can order. **is**
   There _____ that I can order.

7 Mr and Mrs Marsden, take some cake. It's delicious. **help**
   Mr and Mrs Marsden, _____ . It's delicious.

8 Our grandmother gave us this priceless jewellery. **is**
   This priceless jewellery _____ now.

7 Say it! Imagine that you have made some of these things and that some of these things belong to you. Talk to your partner about them.

It's my school bag. It's mine.

I made the cake by myself.

1 **Read.**

We've been to Peru twice. The last time we went, we hiked through the Andes. I don't usually like hiking, but the views were amazing! We're thinking about going to Bolivia next year. Have you ever been to South America?

Review of tenses: present tenses

Present simple

We use the **present simple** to talk about
- general truths.
- things that we do regularly.
- permanent situations.
- timetabled and programmed events in the future.

*I often **watch** documentaries.*
*I **don't** usually **have** breakfast in the morning.*
***Do** you **walk** to school every day?*
*Yes, I **do**. / No, I **don't**.*

Present continuous

We use the **present continuous** to talk about
- actions that are in progress at the time or around the time of speaking.
- actions that are temporary.
- future plans that we have arranged and they usually refer to the near future.
- annoying habits (with **always**, **constantly** and **forever**).
- changing situations.
- what is happening in a picture or photograph.

*Right now, we're **exploring** this unusual site.*
*They **aren't using** the laptop at the moment.*
***Are** you **talking** to me?*
*Yes, I **am**. / No, I'm **not**.*

Review of tenses: present tenses

Present perfect simple

We use the **present perfect simple** to talk about something that
- started in the past but hasn't finished.
- has just finished.
- happened in the past, but we don't know or we don't say exactly when.
- happened in the past but affects the present.

*Daniel **has been** to Peru twice.*
*We **haven't met** our new teacher yet.*

***Have** you ever tried sushi?*
*Yes, I **have**. / No, I **haven't**.*

Present perfect continuous

We use the **present perfect continuous** to talk about
- something that started in the past and is still in progress.
- something that started in the past and has happened repeatedly.
- something that happened in the past and may have finished, but it has a result in the present.
- how long something has been happening from the past up until now.

*My cousins **have been living** in Dubai for two years.*
*Dad **hasn't been travelling** much lately.*
***Have** you **been revising** since this morning?*
*Yes, I **have**. / No, I **haven't**.*

2 **Complete the sentences with a correct present tense. Use the words in brackets.**

1 Right now, we _____'re/are riding_____ camels in the desert. (ride)

2 I _____ around this museum for three hours! (walk)

3 I _____ my best friend tonight. (not meet)

4 The inhabitants _____ the modern building in the town centre. (not like)

5 The express bus to the centre _____ every hour on the hour. (leave)

6 Argh! I _____ a bat before! (never see)

7 We _____ over the Alps at the moment and the view is great! (fly)

8 The sculptor _____ on this statue for six months. (work)

9 _____ a castle? (ever you / visit)

10 The housekeeper _____ the bathroom on a daily basis. (clean)

Review of tenses: past tenses

Past simple

We use the **past simple** to talk about
- actions that started and finished in the past.
- past habits.
- actions that happened one after the other in the past.

*The archaeologists **finished** their research three days ago.*
*Mike **didn't score** a goal in last night's match.*
***Did** you **play** with your friends after school?*
*Yes, I **did**. / No, I **didn't**.*

Past continuous

We use the **past continuous** to
- talk about an action that was in progress at a specific time in the past.
- talk about two or more actions that were in progress at the same time in the past. We use **and** or **while** to connect the actions.
- describe the scene of a story.
- talk about an action in progress in the past that was interrupted by another action.

*At eight o'clock yesterday evening, we **were walking** home from tennis practice.*
*Danielle **wasn't surfing** the Internet while I **was studying**.*
***Were** you **watching** the reality show when I called you?*
*Yes, I **was**. / No, I **wasn't**.*

Review of tenses: past tenses

Past perfect simple

We use the **past perfect simple** to talk about
- something that happened in the past before another action in the past.
- something that happened before a specific time in the past. We often use the word **by** to mean *before* or *not later than*.
- something that happened in the past and had an effect on a later action.

*We **had** never **been** to such a good concert!*
*I **hadn't finished** my homework by the time I went to bed.*
***Had** you **visited** Paris before you went to live there?*
*Yes, I **had**. / No, I **hadn't**.*

Past perfect continuous

We use the **past perfect continuous** to
- emphasise the duration of an action that was in progress before another action or time in the past.
- talk about an action that was in progress in the past, which affected a later action or state.

*Marcia **had been training** hard all day, so she was exhausted in the evening.*
*Unfortunately, I **hadn't been paying** attention during the history lesson!*
***Had** Tony **been reading** about the mysterious disappearance?*
*Yes, he **had**. / No, he **hadn't**.*

3 Circle the correct words.

1 The police **were trying / had been trying** to solve the mystery for a whole year before they found a major clue.

2 Rob **was cooking / cooked** roast beef when I called him last night.

3 While I **got / was getting** on the bus someone bumped into me.

4 Mark got sunburn as he **sat / had been sitting** in the sun all morning.

5 Before I went to Milan, I **had never seen / didn't see** such beautiful boutiques.

6 When she was a teenager, Alice **always wore / had always been wearing** baggy jeans and a T-shirt.

7 While Dalia was walking around the store, she **had come across / came across** the most stylish bag.

8 The music lesson **had already started / already started** when Susie walked in.

Review of tenses: future tenses

Future simple

We use the **future simple**
- to make predictions.
- to talk about decisions we make at the time of speaking.
- to make offers, promises, threats or to give warnings.
- to ask someone to do something for us.
- to state opinions about the future after **think, hope, be sure, believe, bet** and **probably**.

*I promise I'**ll help** you find a solution.*
*We **won't tell** anyone, don't worry.*
***Will** you **take** the dog for a walk for me, please?*
*Yes, I **will**. / No, I **won't**.*

Be going to

We use **be going to**
- to talk about future plans and intentions.
- to predict that something is going to happen when we have proof or information.

*We **are going to do** many things this weekend.*
*They **aren't going to go** to the fashion show.*
***Are** you **going to buy** that silk scarf?*
*Yes, I **am**. / No, **I'm not**.*

Review of tenses: future tenses

Future continuous

We use the **future continuous**
- to talk about something that will be in progress at a specific time in the future.
- to ask politely about someone's future plans.

*In a month's time, **I'll be studying** at Oxford University.*
*Sandra **won't be joining** us on the hike this weekend.*
***Will** Manuela **be working** in her father's company this time next year?*
*Yes, she **will**. / No, she **won't**.*

Future perfect simple

We use the **future perfect simple** to talk about something that will have finished
- before something else happens.
- before a specific time in the future.

*By tomorrow night we'**ll have arrived** home.*
*The film **won't have finished** by eight o'clock.*
***Will** they **have left** by the time I get home?*
*Yes, they **will**. / No, they **won't**.*

Future perfect continuous

We use the **future perfect continuous** to emphasise the duration of an activity that will be in progress before another time or event in the future.

*Next month, we'**ll have been studying** Spanish for a year!*
*I broke my leg and soon, I **won't have been playing** basketball for a month!*
***Will** you **have been teaching** for twenty years next year?*
*Yes, I **will**. / No, I **won't**.*

Note: We can also use the **present simple** and the **present continuous** to talk about the future.

Present simple

We use the **present simple** to talk about timetabled and programmed events in the future.
*The ferry to the island **departs** at eight o'clock in the evening.*
*The school year **doesn't start** in September in Australia.*
***Does** the flight from Los Angeles **arrive** at midnight?*
*Yes, it **does**. / No, it **doesn't**.*

Present continuous

We use the **present continuous** to talk about fixed future plans.
*Sam **is going** out for dinner after work tonight.*
*We **aren't flying** to Madrid tomorrow.*
***Is** Alexander **going** to the party?*
*Yes, he **is**. / No, he **isn't**.*

---

4 Complete the sentences with the correct future tense. Use these verbs.

> buy   depart   do   ~~explore~~   give   meet   start   study

1 This time next month, Joe and I _____ will be exploring _____ South America.
2 Amanda believes she _____ well in her music exams.
3 We must be at the airport by six as our flight to Canada _____ at eight o'clock.
4 Don't worry, I _____ you a lift to the theatre.
5 Hopefully, by this time tomorrow we _____ tickets for the festival.
6 In a week's time, you _____ Spanish for a year!
7 The school year _____ at the beginning of September in the UK.
8 _____ you _____ Maggie after work tonight?

5 **Choose the correct answers.**

1 This time tomorrow, I _____ my project about Egypt.

   a have finished

   (b) will be finishing

   c will finish

2 The ferry to Calais _____ at six thirty in the morning.

   a was departing

   b will have been departing

   c departs

3 Mum _____ a huge fan of classical music since she started studying music at school.

   a was

   b had been

   c has been

4 _____ your history project by the end of the week?

   a Will you have finished

   b We you have finished

   c Did you finish

5 Right now, the Eccleston family _____ in Cairo.

   a will have lived

   b is living

   c have been living

6 Alexander Graham Bell _____ the telephone.

   a invented

   b is inventing

   c will have invented

7 By nine o'clock tonight, we _____ this documentary for two hours!

   a will have been watching

   b are watching

   c will be watching

8 While the divers _____ for treasure, they had an accident.

   a looked

   b had looked

   c were looking

9 Not many people _____ in supernatural powers nowadays.

   a have believed

   b believe

   c will believe

10 We arrived at the port after the cruise ship _____ .

   a has left

   b is leaving

   c had left

11 Don't get up. I _____ you a cup of coffee.

   a is going to get

   b has got

   c will get

12 I'm so tired. We _____ the house for hours.

   a have been cleaning

   b are cleaning

   c will be cleaning

6 **Complete the article with the correct tense. Use the verbs in brackets.**

The Bermuda Triangle

The Bermuda Triangle is a region between Miami, Bermuda and Puerto Rico. Although many years (1) ____have passed____ (pass) since the first disappearance, the Bermuda Triangle (2) _____ (be) still a mystery.

For many years now, planes, vessels and people (3) _____ (disappear) in this area. However, many ships and aircraft continue to (4) _____ (cross) the triangle on a daily basis. One of the many unusual disappearances is the USS Cyclops, which (5) _____ (depart) from Barbados in March 1918, and nobody (6) _____ (see) it since.

Some people (7) _____ (believe) the unusual disappearances are caused by supernatural forces. However, researchers (8) _____ (not agree).

Whatever the cause, the Bermuda Triangle (9) _____ (be) a topic of discussion for many years to come, and in 100 years' time, people (10) _____ (still try) to solve the mystery.

7 Complete the second sentences so they have a similar meaning to the first sentences. Use the words in bold.

1 Jude started studying astronomy six years ago. **been**
  Jude _has been studying astronomy for_ six years.

2 They are going to visit their grandparents this weekend. **visiting**
  They _____ their grandparents this weekend.

3 Emily is still looking for her ring. **found**
  Emily _____ yet.

4 I plan to finish my novel by next year. **have**
  I _____ my novel by next year.

5 Dad made a coffee and then read the newspaper. **after**
  Dad _____ he had made a coffee.

6 I've been staying with my best friend since Monday. **have**
  I _____ with my best friend for five days by Saturday.

7 I think it will be a nice day tomorrow. **rain**
  I _____ tomorrow.

8 This is the first time Maria has written a novel. **never**
  Maria _____ a novel before.

9 My sister and I always have breakfast, and then we go to school. **before**
  My sister and I _____ we go to school.

10 Carla fell asleep on the beach. Then she came out in a rash. **had**
  After Carla _____ on the beach, she came out in a rash.

8 Say it! Talk with your partner about how these things were in the past, how they are now and how you think they'll be in the future. Use these suggestions to help you. Use the appropriate tenses.

- transport
- education
- heating
- cooking
- housing
- free time
- leisure activities
- communication

In the past, most people walked wherever they needed to go.

Nowadays, a lot of people take the bus or the train to reach where they want to go.

1 **Read.**

Oh, thank you! This is such a surprise.

So, such

We use **so** and **such** to give emphasis. **So** is an adverb and we follow it with an adjective without a noun or with another adverb. We can also use **so** before **much** and **many**. **Such** is an adjective and it is followed by another adjective and a noun or just a noun on its own. We can't use **such** before **much** or **many**.

so + adjective
*The Royal Palace at Thebes is **so beautiful**.*

so + adverb
*The baby cried **so loudly** when she fell out of her pram.*

so + much/many + noun
*There are **so many archaeological sites** in Lebanon.*

such + (a/an) + adjective + noun
*We had **such an amazing time** at the funfair.*

such + noun
*The expedition was **such a success**.*

Note: We can replace **such** + **a/an** + adjective + noun with **so** + adjective + **a/an** + noun.
*It was **such a strange place** that I felt scared.*
*It was **so strange a place** that I felt scared.*

2 **Complete the sentences with *so* or *such*.**

1   It was _____so_____ incredibly hot in the desert that we couldn't even walk.
2   Marilyn is _____ a stylish model.
3   He was _____ persuasive a person that we bought the house without thinking twice!
4   Lilly is _____ a wonderful painter.
5   I can't believe you are _____ superficial.
6   The Loch Ness Monster is still _____ a mystery.
7   Mandy has _____ many computer games.
8   The works of Gaudí are _____ unusual.

3 **Choose the correct answers.**

1 €100 for a pair of shoes! I can't believe they're _____ .
   a so expensive *(circled)*
   b such expensive
   c such an expensive

2 It was _____ last night that I couldn't sleep.
   a such a hot
   b so hot a
   c so hot

3 Kelly is _____ girl!
   a so clever
   b such a clever
   c clever

4 It was _____ train, it went from Melbourne to Sydney in only six hours.
   a so fast
   b such a fast
   c fast

5 We aren't going to play the game tonight. We have got _____ homework to do.
   a such
   b so much
   c so many

6 Josh and Melinda are _____ children!
   a so noisy
   b such noisy
   c such a noisy

7 How could you say _____ thing to your brother?
   a awful
   b such an awful
   c so awful

8 I can't believe that Peter lied to his parents. He is usually _____ boy.
   a so good
   b such a good
   c such good

4 **Complete the sentences with *so* or *such (a/an)* and these words.**

> cheap   efficient   ~~frightening~~   fun   heavy   high   intelligent   waste

1 The film was _____*so frightening*_____ that the viewers couldn't watch it!
2 Melanie is _____ employee that she always gets a bonus.
3 The rain was _____ that the match was postponed.
4 We had _____ at the funfair that we didn't stop laughing.
5 It was _____ mountain that the climber couldn't reach the top.
6 The designer clothes were _____ in the sales that I bought lots of new dresses.
7 The professor is _____ person.
8 The meeting was _____ of time.

5 **Circle the correct words.**

1 The music is **so**/**such** loud! I wish they would turn it down.
2 She spoke **so quickly / quickly** that I couldn't understand what she was saying.
3 The investigation was **such / so** a disaster.
4 I can't believe that the furniture is **such / so** expensive.
5 It was **such a luxurious / so luxurious** hotel that I didn't want to leave.
6 The children had **so enjoyable / such an enjoyable** time at the party.
7 The food last night was **such / so** awful that I couldn't eat any of it.
8 We had **so / such a** wonderful time in New York that I wish we could move there.

6 Complete the second sentences so they have a similar meaning to the first sentences. Use the words in bold.

1 My day was so busy that I didn't have time to have lunch. **such**

I had _____such a busy day that_____ I didn't have time to have lunch.

2 Marsa Matruh has got such nice beaches we are thinking of going back next year. **nice**

The beaches in Marsa Matruh _____ we are thinking of going back next year.

3 The book about space travel was so fascinating I couldn't put it down! **such**

It was _____ that I couldn't put it down.

4 It was such a boring presentation that some of the participants fell asleep. **was**

The presentation _____ that some of the participants fell asleep.

5 The journey was so incredible that I'd like to go on a similar one again. **an**

It was _____ that I'd like to go on a similar one again.

6 Hannah spoke to the head teacher in such a rude way that she was given detention. **so**

Hannah spoke to _____ that she was given detention.

7 The comedy was so funny that I couldn't stop laughing. **such**

It was _____ that I couldn't stop laughing.

8 Pilates is such a relaxing activity that I've decided to practise it regularly. **so**

Pilates is _____ that I've decided to practise it regularly.

7 Say it! Talk to your partner about these things. Use *so*, *such* and these suggestions to help you.

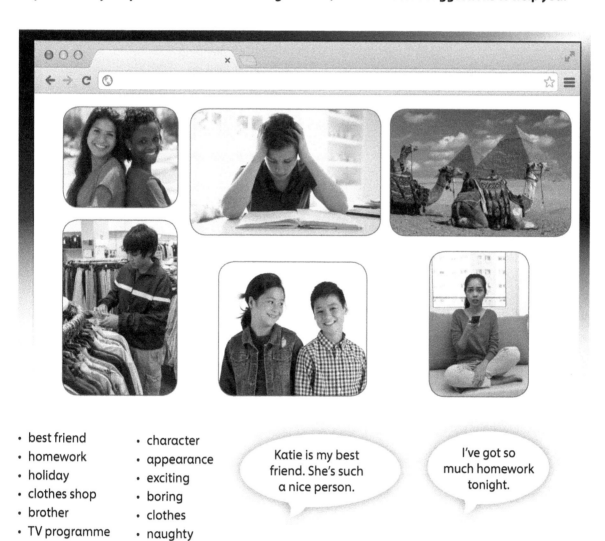

- best friend
- homework
- holiday
- clothes shop
- brother
- TV programme
- character
- appearance
- exciting
- boring
- clothes
- naughty

> Katie is my best friend. She's such a nice person.

> I've got so much homework tonight.

1 **Put the adjectives in brackets in the correct order and complete the sentences.**

1 Helen bought me some _____ nice black leather _____ gloves. (leather / black / nice)

2 Who made that _____ statue? (grey / awful / old)

3 My cousins stayed in a _____ cottage. (little / white / stunning)

4 Dalia was wearing a(n) _____ hat at the fashion show last night. (straw / big / unusual)

5 Have you seen my _____ purse? (velvet / tiny / green)

6 I'm going to buy that _____ watch later on today. (silver / gorgeous / Swiss)

2 **Choose the correct answers.**

1 The weather is getting _____ every year.
   a warmer
   b the warmest
   c warmest

2 Are diamonds _____ than pearls?
   a the most expensive
   b more expensive
   c as expensive as

3 I arrived at the castle _____ than you.
   a the earliest
   b early
   c earlier

4 Thomas speaks English _____ of all the students in the class.
   a the least fluently
   b less fluently
   c as fluently as

5 Unfortunately, we weren't _____ as we had thought.
   a the best prepared
   b better prepared
   c as well prepared

6 What is _____ thing in the world?
   a most important
   b the most important
   c as important as

7 In my opinion, solar power is _____ wind power.
   a more efficient
   b as efficient as
   c the most efficient

8 I find cross country racing _____ .
   a challenged
   b challenging
   c challenge

9 The more I read about the solar system, _____ I want to learn about space.
   a more than
   b the more
   c the most

10 I am quite _____ by the number of disappearances in the area.
   a to disturb
   b disturbed
   c disturbing

3 **Complete the sentences. Use these words.**

enough   excitedly   later   outside   so   yesterday

1 It's a beautiful day today. Let's have lunch _____ outside _____ .

2 Tamara walked into the oral exam _____ confidently.

3 I feel better today than I did _____ .

4 Will they be dropping in _____ on today?

5 The children waved _____ at Mickey Mouse.

6 I can't act well _____ to become an actor.

4 Complete the sentences with adjectives ending in *–ing* or *–ed* formed from the words in brackets.

1 I was so _____ frightened _____ that I couldn't sleep. (frighten)

2 Running cross country is very _____ . (tire)

3 The film was so _____ that I couldn't keep my eyes open. (bore)

4 The children really enjoyed the performance. They were thoroughly _____ . (amuse)

5 The actor felt _____ when he forgot his words. (embarrass)

6 I think learning about other cultures is really _____ . (interest)

7 I love going on rollercoaster rides. It's so _____ . (excite)

8 Lyn was _____ to hear the good news. (thrill)

5 The words in bold are wrong. Write the correct words.

1 I'd like **nobody** to tell me the origins of this theory, please.   _____ somebody _____

2 Are the singers going to write the lyrics by **ourselves**?   _____

3 Is this black leather jacket **your**?   _____

4 There was **anything** interesting in the newspaper, so I threw it away.   _____

5 I was really tired because **anybody** helped me with the bags.   _____

6 I was in a huge castle all by **me**.   _____

7 I don't have black sunglasses. They aren't **my**.   _____

8 Josh wants to decorate his room all by **him**.   _____

6 Complete the dialogue with the correct tense. Use the verbs in brackets.

Nina: Harry, I (1) _____ 'm/am thinking _____ (think) of writing an article on the Loch Ness Monster.
(2) _____ (you / believe) there is any truth in it?

Harry: I (3) _____ (not know).

Nina: Well, the modern myth all started in 1933. A local couple, the Spicers, (4) _____
(drive) along Loch Ness, which is a long narrow deep lake in Scotland, when they
(5) _____ (see) a large creature crossing the road in front of them. Since then,
people (6) _____ (try) to take pictures of it. It's weird that before 1933, nobody
(7) _____ (ever spot) it, isn't it?

Harry: Yes, that's true.

Nina: Anyhow, in 1934, R K Wilson claimed that he (8) _____ (take) a photo of Nessie.

Harry: Nessie?

Nina: Yes, the monster is often referred to as Nessie.

Harry: Mm. Most scientists (9) _____ (believe) that it's a myth, though.

Nina: Yes, they do. However, I (10) _____ (think) that in 100 years' time, people
(11) _____ (still investigate) the mystery. So, myth or no myth, for
years to come, it (12) _____ (always be) fascinating.

7 Complete the sentences with *so* or *such*.

1 Marcia is _____ so _____ kind that I really like her!
2 You have _____ bad an attitude that you'll never succeed.
3 Mozart was _____ a great composer!
4 You're wearing _____ beautiful cowboy boots.
5 Bagpipes are _____ fascinating!
6 Dad is _____ a spontaneous person; he never plans ahead.
7 The film was _____ funny that I couldn't stop laughing.
8 It was _____ a boring book that he never finished it.

WRITING PROJECT

8 Look at a project about the Great Pyramid of Giza. Circle the correct words.

A marvellous mystery

The (1) **huge ancient Egyptian** / **Egyptian ancient huge** Great Pyramid of Giza, which (2) **also knows /
is also known** as the Cheops Pyramid, is the largest of the three pyramids and the oldest of the Seven Wonders of
the Ancient World. It (3) **used to / is used to** be the tallest man-made structure in the world and it remains one of
the most (4) **fascinated / fascinating** in history. However, many details about its construction remain a mystery.

People (5) **believe / are believing** that the Great Pyramid
was built as a tomb for Cheops the Pharaoh, by Cheops'
highest official, Hemon, and that construction lasted between
14 and 20 years. However, there is still mystery surrounding
its construction. Even today, (6) **anybody / nobody** is sure of
the techniques used to build the pyramid. The theory that
huge blocks of limestone (7) **have been moved / were moved**
from a quarry and then put into place is the most
(8) **convincing / convinced**. Even its original height is
(9) **rather uncertain / uncertain rather**. Another mystery
is who (10) **was the pyramid built / did the pyramid built** by?
According to the Ancient Greeks, slaves built the pyramid,
while modern Egyptologists (11) **insist / are insisting** that
skilled workers (12) **employed / were employed**.

9 Now it's your turn to do a project about a mysterious construction. Find or draw a picture of
it and write about it.

Irregular verbs

Infinitive	Past simple	Past participle
be	was/were	been
become	became	become
begin	began	begun
bet	bet	bet
bite	bit	bitten
break	broke	broken
bring	brought	brought
build	built	built
burn	burnt	burnt
buy	bought	bought
catch	caught	caught
choose	chose	chosen
come	came	come
cost	cost	cost
cut	cut	cut
die	died	died
dig	dug	dug
do	did	done
draw	drew	drawn
drink	drank	drunk
drive	drove	driven
eat	ate	eaten
fall	fell	fallen
feed	fed	fed
feel	felt	felt
fight	fought	fought
find	found	found
fly	flew	flown
forget	forgot	forgotten
freeze	froze	frozen
get	got	got
give	gave	given
go	went	gone
grow	grew	grown
have	had	had
hear	heard	heard
hide	hid	hidden
hit	hit	hit
hold	held	held
hurt	hurt	hurt
keep	kept	kept

Infinitive	Past simple	Past participle
know	knew	known
learn	learnt	learnt
leave	left	left
lend	lent	lent
let	let	let
lie	lay	lain
lose	lost	lost
make	made	made
mean	meant	meant
meet	met	met
pay	paid	paid
put	put	put
read	read	read
ride	rode	ridden
ring	rang	rung
run	ran	run
say	said	said
see	saw	seen
sell	sold	sold
send	sent	sent
shoot	shot	shot
show	showed	shown
sing	sang	sung
sit	sat	sat
sleep	slept	slept
smell	smelt	smelt
speak	spoke	spoken
spend	spent	spent
stand	stood	stood
steal	stole	stolen
swim	swam	swum
take	took	taken
teach	taught	taught
tell	told	told
think	thought	thought
throw	threw	thrown
understand	understood	understood
wake	woke	woken
wear	wore	worn
win	won	won
write	wrote	written

NATIONAL GEOGRAPHIC
L E A R N I N G

National Geographic Learning,
a Cengage Company

Wonderful World 6 **Grammar Book,
Second Edition**

Vice President, Editorial Director: John McHugh

Executive Editors: Eugenia Corbo, Siân Mavor

Commissioning Editor: Kayleigh Buller

Head of Strategic Marketing EMEA ELT:
   Charlotte Ellis

Product Marketing Executive: Ellen Setterfield

Head of Production and Design: Celia Jones

Content Project Manager: Melissa Beavis

Manufacturing Manager: Eyvett Davis

Art Director: Brenda Carmichael

Cover Design: Lisa Trager

Interior Design and Composition:
   Lumina Datamatics, Inc.

For permission to use material from this text or product, submit all requests online at **cengage.com/permissions**
Further permissions questions can be emailed to
permissionrequest@cengage.com

Grammar Book: Level 6
ISBN: 978-1-4737-6085-1

National Geographic Learning
Cheriton House, North Way
Andover, Hampshire, SP10 5BE
United Kingdom

Locate your local office at **international.cengage.com/region**

Visit National Geographic Learning online at **NGL.Cengage.com/ELT**
Visit our corporate website at **www.cengage.com**

Printed in the United Kingdom by Ashford Colour Press
Print Number: 02 Print Year: 2020

MIX
Paper from
responsible sources
FSC® C011748